A PRACTICAL GUIDE TO
GARDENING

First Published in 1998

This edition Published in 1998 by
Brockhampton Press,
a member of Hodder Headline PLC Group,
20 Bloomsbury Street,
London WC1 B3QA

Specialist Authors:	Mary Moody
	Rosa Vallance
	Moira Ryan
	Bruce Harkness
	Hugh Redgrove
Photography supplied by:	Harry Smith, horticultural photographic collection
Editor:	Peter Leek
Colour Separation:	GA Graphics

Printed in Singapore by Imago

Title: GARDENING
ISBN: 1-86019-414-1

A PRACTICAL GUIDE TO GARDENING

A practical and essential guide to all your gardening requirements.

BROCKHAMPTON PRESS

CONTENTS

CONTENTS

INTRODUCTION

For anybody planning a new garden or refurbishing an old one, this book will provide practical advice and a guide to an array of techniques and and gardening ideas. From the creation of the popular herbaceous border and the rose garden, to the rewards of the herb garden and vegetable patch.

The 'Annuals and Biennials' section contains all you need to know about growing these popular garden bedding and show pieces, listing suitable plants and explaining when, where and how to sow them. There are individual sections on plants grown for hanging baskets, rock gardens and greenhouses as well as climbing annuals and the important F1 Hybrids.

In 'Perennials' the popular herbaceous border is investigated and there is an array of advice for growing a wide range of perennial plants for this popular garden treatment. Soil improvement and garden maintenance, to ensure a healthy and productive garden, is foremost in the practices described in each section, especially in 'Vegetables' where you are taken through the methods of crop rotation and companion planting.

In 'Roses' you learn how to begin growing roses and then how to get the best from them. Beginning with an explanation of the various types and how to chooses suitable roses and lay out a rose garden. With important information on pruning and protection from pests and diseases you are provided with sound advice for growing this, often neglected, favourite plant.

The term 'bulb' covers a multitude of plants such as corms, tubers and rhizomes. All of these are included in the 'Bulbs' section where you learn how to incorporate them successfully into a garden by naturalising them in lawns, planting them as part of an herbaceous border or making a strong statement in a garden bed or rockery.

Herbs in the garden are a double delight, making an attractive display of subtle foliage and providing a continuous supply of ingredients for the kitchen. Whether you want to grow them in pots, or in a traditional style herb garden the comprehensive guide in the 'Herbs' section will answer the needs of anyone interested in herb gardening.

Right: A healthy vegetable patch protected by a traditional scarecrow.

ANNUALS
AND
BIENNIALS

WHAT ARE ANNUALS AND BIENNIALS?

True annuals are plants that will complete their life cycle within twelve months of sowing. Biennials require two growing seasons to do so and are usually sown in summer to flower during the following spring and summer.

Many other plants that botanists would define as perennial can be treated as annuals – although some are half-hardy and, while able to flower well for a single season, are not hardy enough to be used for more than one year. An example is the brilliant-scarlet *Salvia splendens*. Half-hardy annuals are generally raised in a greenhouse, then 'pricked out' (transplanted, a few centimetres apart, in larger boxes) and grown under protection before being planted out.

BIENNIALS

The winter hardiness of biennials depends on the district where they are to be grown (local advice should be sought regarding plants such as *Begonia semperflorens*, browallia and *Primula malacoïdes*). But there are significant advantages in planting out in late summer or autumn for all those hardy enough to winter well. For example, Canterbury bells (*Campanula medium*) that are planted outside as transplants in the autumn will flower well the following summer, but if planted out in the spring they tend not to flower until twelve months later! Sweet Williams behave in a similar way.

Biennials are usually sown in a seedbed in the open, or in boxes in a frame or greenhouse, and transplanted as seedlings. They are then put in their final quarters in late autumn, as in the case of wallflowers (*Cheiranthus cheiri*) – which do best in cool regions – and double daisies (*Bellis*). It is quite important to plant out forget-me-nots (*Myosotis*) and cinerarias in the autumn, as both of these flower early and therefore need to be planted out well ahead of flowering time.

Cinerarias are suitable only for areas free from frost – but in such areas they are very showy, and they are particularly useful for shady gardens. There are short, medium and tall types, and the colour range is wide. Especially good are the rich blue shades.

Plants that are not frost hardy include *Begonia semperflorens*, coleus (grown for their foliage colour), dahlias (which have perennial tubers) and impatiens. The latter have become extremely popular plants. They are available in both short and taller varieties; and also in numerous double-flowered cultivars, which are mainly propagated by cuttings. Impatiens grow well in full sun if watered, or in shade, and are popular container plants for patios.

Below: Bellis perennis 'Pomponette'.

Below: Mixed impatiens.

Left: Begonia semperflorens.

HARDY BIENNIALS

These are plants that are sown the year before they are expected to flower. They are raised in a seedbed outdoors or in a cool, shady frame and may be thinned out or transplanted when large enough. For best results, planting out should be done in autumn; if you buy them from your garden centre in punnets or seedling trays, plant them out early in the season. Even in areas where the winters are mild, planting at that colder time will result in smaller flowering plants, except perhaps with pansies and violas.

The following table lists some popular hardy biennials.

Right: Digitalis purpurea.

			SUN ✱ PARTIAL SHADE ○ SHADE ●				
NAME	COLOURS	HEIGHT IN CM	SUN OR SHADE	SOW OUTDOORS	SOW IN BOXES	TIME OF SOWING	REMARKS
Bellis (double daisy)	various	15	✱ ○	✔		Summer/Autumn	transplant
Browallia 'Jingle Bells'	mixed	40	○	✔		Autumn/Spring	transplant, warm regions
Campanula medium (Canterbury bells)		30-60	✱ ○		✔	Summer	transplant
Cheiranthus cheiri (wallflower)	gold, orange, primrose, red	40	✱	✔	✔	Autumn	cool regions
Dianthus barbatus (Sweet William)	salmon	30	✱ ○	✔	✔	Summer	often perennial
Digitalis (foxglove)	cream, pink, purple	100	✱	✔	✔	Summer/Autumn	
Ersimum hieraciifolium (Siberian wallflower)	bright orange	30	✱	✔		Autumn	cool regions
Lunaria (honesty)	white, purple	75	✱ ○	✔		Summer	difficult to transplant
Matthiola (Brompton stock)	various	35	✱		✔	Summer	scented
Myosotis (forget-me-not)	blue, white	15-20	✱ ○	✔		Summer/Autumn	
Pansy and viola	various	15-20	✱ ○	✔	✔	Summer/Autumn	
Primula malacoïdes	white, pink, crimson.	40	✱ ○		✔	Summer	warm regions
Primula obconica	white, blue, pink, red	35	✱ ○		✔	Summer	warm regions
Primula vulgaris elatior (polyanthus)	white, pink, yellow, crimson	15-25	✱ ○		✔	Summer/Autumn	perennial or biennial
Rudbeckia hirta gloriosa (black-eyed Susan)	yellow, orange, bronze	45-90	○		✔	Autumn	long-lasting flowers, single and double
Verbena	bright colours	30	○	✔	✔	Spring	spreading

ANNUALS

Shallow seed drills

EASY-TO-GROW ANNUALS

Annuals that can be sown directly in well-prepared flowerbeds and which come quickly into flower are bound to be popular if they are capable of sustaining flowering for a lengthy period. There are numerous suitable varieties to choose from. In a few cases they must be sown in situ, but in most cases (unless otherwise noted) they may be sown in boxes and transplanted – an arrangement that permits a faster succession of blooms after early-flowering annuals or bulbs have finished.

Below: Calendula (Fiesta series) 'Gitana'.

Before sowing time, prepare the growing site. If the soil is lumpy and heavy, compost should be worked in and planting mix applied to the surface. Then choose a dry day, apply a little general fertiliser, and rake it in. Seed can be broadcast, or it can be sown in shallow drills about 8 cm apart. If sowing is in drills, it will be possible to keep down seedling weed with a small hand hoe, which is quicker than hand weeding. Cover seed rows with soil; or if the seed is broadcast, rake it in. After germination, some thinning may be necessary.

Some seedlings can be safely transplanted, but the following do not transplant easily: clarkia, eschscholzia, godetia, gypsophila, linaria, *Linum grandiflorum* 'Rubrum', nigella, *Phlox drummondii* and poppies. Remember that if annuals need staking it is far better to support them with twiggy stakes while they are still erect, and that the removal of spent flowers will prolong flowering and improve the plant's appearance.

The following table gives a selection of popular hardy annuals.

| NAME | COLOURS | HEIGHT IN CM | SUN ❋ PARTIAL SHADE ◐ SHADE ● | | | | |
			SUN OR SHADE	SOW OUTDOORS	SOW IN BOXES	TIME OF SOWING	REMARKS
Calendula (marigold)	yellow, red, orange	30-45	❋	✔	✔	Summer/Autumn	
Clarkia elegans	white, pink	60	❋	✔		Spring	sow in situ
Cleome (spider flower)	pink, mauve, white	90	❋		✔	Spring	
Cornflower	white, pink, red, blue	25-90	❋ ◐	✔	✔	Autumn	cool regions
Cosmos (daisy-like)	white, pink, crimson	90	❋	✔		Spring	
Delphinium 'Imperial Double'	white, salmon, pink, red	120	❋	✔	✔	Autumn only	cool regions only
Dimorphotheca	pink, white, yellow	10-20	❋	✔		Spring	light soil
Eschscholzia	various	30	❋	✔		Spring	sow in situ
Godetia azaleaflora	various	40	❋	✔		Spring	sow in situ
Godetia 'Sybil Sherwood'	salmon-edged white	45	❋	✔		Spring	sow in situ
Gypsophila	white, rose	40-45	❋	✔		Spring	sow in situ
Helichrysum	wide colour range	75	❋	✔	✔	Spring	sow in situ
Helipterum roseum	double mixed, white, rose	30	❋	✔		Spring	
Iberis (candytuft)	'Fairy Mixed', 'Giant White'	20-30	❋	✔	✔	Autumn	
Lathyrus vernus (sweet pea) 'Bijou Dwarf'	various	30	❋	✔	✔	Autumn/Spring	no staking needed
Lathyrus odoratus (sweet pea) climbing	various	175	❋	✔	✔	Autumn/Spring	scented
Lavatera (mallow)	white, pink, rose	60-90	❋	✔	✔	Winter/Spring	
Limnanthes douglasii	white, yellow	15	❋		✔	Spring	

NAME	COLOURS	HEIGHT IN CM	SUN ✲ PARTIAL SHADE ◯ SHADE ● SUN OR SHADE	SOW OUTDOORS	SOW IN BOXES	TIME OF SOWING	REMARKS
Limonium sinuatum	white, blue, pink, yellow	45	✲	✔	✔	Spring	sow early in boxes
Linaria (toadflax)	various	22	✲	✔		Spring	sow in situ
Linum grandiflorum 'Rubrum' (red annual flax)	red	30	✲	✔		Spring	sow in situ
Lobularia maritima	white, rose, purple	15	✲ ◯	✔		Spring/Any time	often self-seeds
Lychnis viscaria	white, pink, red, blue mix	30	✲	✔		Spring	
Nigella damascena (love-in-a-mist)	rose, blue, white	35	✲	✔		Spring	sow in situ
Papaver 'Shirley' (poppy)	wide colour range	60	✲	✔		Spring	sow in situ
Psylliostachys suworowii	pink spikes	70	✲	✔		Spring	sow early in boxes
Reseda 'Machet Rubin' (mignonette)	reddish colours	40	✲	✔		Spring	sow in situ
Scabiosa	white, pink, red, blue	45-90	✲	✔	✔	Spring	

Far right:
Papaver nudicaule.

Right: Eschscholzias.

HALF-HARDY ANNUALS

These are the kinds of annuals that must be raised in a frame or greenhouse, or in a few cases sown outdoors after the danger of frost has passed. The majority are more easily raised in a greenhouse.

Germination time varies, and most kinds require pricking out into boxes or pots of potting compost. If you wish to avoid this chore, you can use small peat pots, sowing a few seeds in each; once the plants are strong enough and have been hardened off (allowing a gradual lowering of the temperature), they can be transplanted intact, pot and all, to their flowering positions.

Some of the seeds – such as those of lobelia, begonias and petunias – are very small. These need to be sown carefully and quite thinly, with little or no soil covering, and kept out of direct sunlight. They must not be allowed to dry out, even on the surface; but you can enclose the pots in large clear-plastic bags, which must be removed as soon as germination is complete.

Nowadays the numerous garden centres often do all this work for you, offering a good range of these plants in punnets ready for planting out. But it may well be that you want to use seed collected from your own garden, or wish to grow varieties unavailable in punnets. In any case, you will find that raising your own seedlings can add a great deal of interest to your gardening.

The following table gives a selection of popular half-hardy annuals.

Below: Nicotiana 'Lime Green'.

SUN ☼ PARTIAL SHADE ○ SHADE ●

NAME	COLOURS	HEIGHT IN CM	SUN OR SHADE	SOW OUTDOORS	SOW IN BOXES	TIME OF SOWING	REMARKS
Ageratum	blue, pink	20	☼ ○	✔	✔	Spring	avoid frost
Amaranthus caudatus (love-lies-bleeding)	red spikes	50	☼	✔	✔	Spring	
Antirrhinum (snapdragon) tall, intermediate, dwarf	various	35-75	☼ ○		✔	Winter/Spring	cool site required in warm regions
Aster (single, double)	various	22-60	☼ ○	✔	✔	Spring	stake tall varieties
Begonia	white, pink, scarlet	15-30	☼ ○		✔	Spring	sow thinly
Dianthus caryophyllus (carnation)	various/mixed	45	☼		✔	Autumn	transplant
Chrysanthemum 'Korean Rainbow'	various	60-80	☼		✔	Spring/Autumn	transplant
Cineraria	blue, white, purple, crimson	20-60	○ ●	✔	✔	Autumn	frost tender, good in pots
Coleus	various foliage colours	20-90	☼ ○		✔	Spring	frost tender
Euphorbia marginata (snow-on-the-mountain)	green and white foliage	60	☼		✔	Spring	
Geranium 'Summer Showers'	various	30	☼		✔	Winter	trailing habit
Impatiens	various	15-30	☼ ○		✔	Spring	also double and bicolour, frost tender
Lobelia erinus	blue, pink, white	20	☼		✔	Spring	sow thinly
Lobelia erinus pendula (trailing lobelia)	blue shades	15-30	☼		✔	Spring	sow thinly
Mesembryanthemum criniflorum (Livingstone daisy)	apricot, crimson, pink	8	☼	✔	✔	Spring	prefers dry soil

NAME	COLOURS	HEIGHT IN CM	SUN ☀ PARTIAL SHADE ◐ SHADE ● SUN OR SHADE	SOW OUTDOORS	SOW IN BOXES	TIME OF SOWING	REMARKS
emesia 'Carnival'	mixed/various	22	☀	✔	✔	Autumn/Spring	
icotiana (tobacco plant)	white, green red, pink	22-90	☀	✔	✔	Spring	
etunia 'Cascade' ery large single	mixed	30	☀		✔	Spring	sow thinly, suits planters and baskets
ery large double	various	30	☀		✔	Spring	sow thinly, compact habit
Colour Parade'	mixed	60	☀		✔	Spring	sow thinly, transplant when small
blox drummondii	mixed/various	20-35	☀	✔	✔	Autumn/Spring	does not transplant well
ortulaca	mixed	15	☀	✔	✔	Spring	usually semi-double
alvia farinacea 'Victoria'	violet-blue spikes	45	☀		✔	Spring	long-lasting blooms
alvia splendens	scarlet, pink, white, purple	30-45	☀		✔	Spring	scarlet is best known
agetes 'Gem'	lemon, orange	15	☀		✔	Spring	single flowers, fine 'lacy' foliage
agetes erecta frican marigold	primrose, gold, orange	20-35	☀		✔	Spring	usually double flowers
agetes erecta rench marigold	gold, orange, brown, lemon	15-20	☀		✔	Spring	
innia elegans	mixed/various	60	☀		✔	Spring	transplant
nvy	chartreuse green	75	☀		✔	Spring	plant after frost
Giant Dahlia'	mixed	75	☀		✔	Spring	plant after frost

PLANTS FOR THE GREENHOUSE

If you have a greenhouse, you can grow many annuals and biennials to flower in winter, or at least earlier in spring than when grown outdoors.

If the greenhouse can be moderately heated in the winter, then the range of suitable plants will be wider – especially in areas where frosts are heavier than just a few degrees below zero. To avoid lanky growth, close attention must be paid to watering and ventilation (the amount of care varies, depending on the local climate and maximum light available in winter).

Below: Antirrhinum.

FOR UNHEATED GREENHOUSES

Anchusa 'Blue Angel' – long sprays; rich, deep blue; 25 cm; sow in spring.

Antirrhinum – various colours and heights; dwarf varieties for pots; sow in late winter/early spring.

Calendula 'Fiesta' – dwarf; yellow and orange; 30 cm; sow in summer/autumn.

Centaurea (cornflower) 'Baby Blue' – bushy; rich, deep blue; 25 cm; sow in autumn.

Godetia 'Salmon Prince' – pink overlaid with orange; 30 cm; sow in spring.

Delphinium (larkspur) – mixed; 30 cm.

Lathyrus odoratus (sweet pea) 'Bijou Dwarf' – mixed; 30 cm; sow in autumn.

Petunia 'Cascade' – various colours; 30 cm; superb for tubs and hanging baskets; sow in spring.

Primula vulgaris elatior (polyanthus) 'Crescendo' – superb mixture; 15-20 cm; shade in summer; sow late autumn.

Primula vulgaris (primrose) 'Spectrum Mixed' – fine colour range; 15 cm; shade in summer; sow late autumn.

Malcolmia maritima (Virginian stock) 'East Lothian' – compact; mixed colours; 45 cm; cool regions; sow in early autumn.

Tagetes (marigold) 'Red Cherry' – bright orange red; 30 cm; well-suited to pots; sow in autumn.

FOR FROST-FREE GREENHOUSES

Begonia semperflorens – white, pink, rose, scarlet; 15-30 cm; sow in spring.

Browallia 'Jingle Bells' – 5 cm flowers; various shades; 40 cm; sow in autumn/spring.

Calceolaria 'Mixed Colours' – yellow to red; 25 cm; sow in summer.

Chrysanthemum 'Charm Mixed' – 40-50 cm; suitable for pots; sow in Spring.

Cineraria – dwarf; various colours; 20 cm; sow in summer.

Coleus 'Rainbow Mixed' – for foliage colour; 30-50 cm; sow in spring.

Impatiens 'Accent Strain' – many colours; dwarf, 15 cm; sow in spring.

Primula malacoïdes – white, pink, red; 40 cm; flowers in August; sow in summer.

Primula obconica – white, blue, pink, salmon, red; 35 cm; sow in summer.

Schizanthus 'Star Parade' – multicoloured; compact; 45 cm; sow in summer.

Right: A colourful display of Begonia semperflorens.

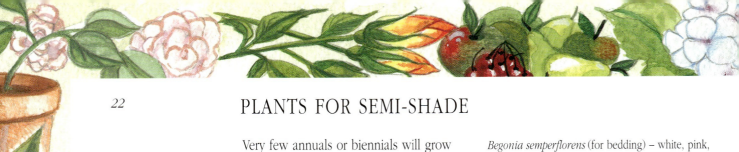

PLANTS FOR SEMI-SHADE

Very few annuals or biennials will grow in dense shade, particularly under ever-green trees. In part-shade where the soil is moderately fertile and there is some sun for part of the day, some annuals will give a reasonable display.

Below: Canterbury bells (Campanula medium).

Ageratum – blue, pink; 20 cm; sow in spring.
Anchusa 'Blue Angel' – blue; 25 cm; sow in spring.

Begonia semperflorens (for bedding) – white, pink, red; 15-25 cm; sow in seed trays.
Bellis (double daisy) – various colours; 15 cm; sow in summer/autumn.
Browallia 'Jingle Bells' – mixed colours; 40 cm; sow in autumn/spring.
Campanula medium (Canterbury bells) – blue, pink, white; 30-60 cm; sow under glass in late spring and plant in early summer.
Lobelia – blue, buff, apricot, crimson, pink, white; 15 cm; sow thinly in trays in spring.
Lobularia maritima – white, pink, purple; 15 cm; sow at any time.
Mimulus – mixed, orange and yellow; 20 cm; prefers moist soil; sow in seed trays.
Myosotis (forget-me-not) – blue shades, white; 15-20 cm; sow in summer/autumn.
Nicotiana (tobacco plant) – white, pink, red, green; 22-90 cm; sow in Spring.
Nigella damascena (love-in-a-mist) – white, blue, pink shades; 35 cm; sow in situ in early spring.
Viola x wittrockiana (pansy) and violas – various colours, especially F1 Hybrids; 15-20 cm; sow in summer/early autumn.
Phlox drummondii – mixed, wide colour range; 20-35 cm; sow autumn/spring.

HANGING BASKETS

Hanging baskets provide a simple and attractive way of decorating a porch or terrace during the summer; they may also be used in the greenhouse. Both annuals and biennials can play an important part.

Baskets are mostly made from stout galvanised wire, in various sizes. Others are made from plastic mesh. Each basket should first be lined with sphagnum moss (A); alternatively, polythene can be used as a lining, with holes punched in the base for drainage. For larger baskets it is possible to combine these two linings (B) – which has the advantage of reducing watering while retaining a pleasing appearance.

Use a good potting compost, with the addition of a slow-action fertiliser. Planting should be done with well-established plants just coming into flower. Put the larger plants into place first; then the smaller plants (C), such as trailing lobelia and alyssum, can be tucked in between. Geraniums, both the erect zonal types and the trailing ivy-leaf types, are popular long-flowering plants. The following annuals and biennials are also suitable:

ageratum, *Begonia semperflorens*, browallia, gypsophila, nemesia, petunias (especially the 'Cascade' varieties), trailing lobelia, trailing nasturtiums and verbena. With trailing nasturtiums, you can push seeds into the compost at planting time.

During warm weather one must be prepared to water baskets every day, but there are watering nozzles available which are designed to avoid having to bring the basket down for watering. After watering, hanging baskets are very heavy – so make sure that they are hung from strong hooks.

Baskets should be placed in positions where they do not get full sun during the hottest part of the day, but where they are not in deep shade.

A

B

C

DRYING ANNUALS AND BIENNIALS

There are a number of annuals and biennials that are ideal for drying. They also add colour to mixed borders while growing, before being used for indoor winter decoration. Some have interesting seed pods that can be dried for decorative purposes.

Unless otherwise stated, these seeds are usually sown under glass, allowing about six weeks for development before they are planted out; but it is also possible, in warm regions on light soils, to sow the seeds direct in sunny positions and thin them out as required.

The flower stems should generally be cut just before the flowers are fully developed, tied in small bunches and hung upside down in a warm, dry, airy room.

Helipterum roseum – mixed, white, pink, rose; large-flowered; 45 cm.

Helichrysum bracteatum 'Monstrosum' – white, pink, yellow, crimson; double daisies that have incurving petals; tall to 90 cm; dwarf 30 cm; always cut in bud for drying.

Lunaria (honesty) – white, purple flowers; silvery seed pods; 75 cm.

Molucella laevis (bells of Ireland) – green flower bracts on graceful stems; they turn straw-coloured when dried; 70 cm.

Nigella damascena (love-in-a-mist) – rose, blue, white; inflated seed capsules; 35 cm.

Limonium sinuatum – white, yellow, blue, rose; flat flowerheads; up to 45 cm; plant out on light soils in autumn.

Psylliostachys suworowii (statice, pink rats' tails) – delightful graceful pink spikes; up to 70 cm; sow in early spring. There are several perennial varieties.

Xeranthemum annuum – white, pink, mauve, purple; easy to grow; 45 cm.

CLIMBING ANNUALS

There are a number of climbers that are rapid growers, ideal for quickly covering fences, trellises, walls or tree stumps.

Sweet peas and scarlet runner beans are favourites. Both need sites that have been well prepared by deep digging and the addition of good compost or well-rotted animal manure. It is usually necessary to provide netting (either plastic or wire) which is stretched out, or wound around a tree stump.

The tender climbers – both half-hardy annuals (HHA) and half-hardy perennials (HHP) – should be sown under glass and planted out when frosts are over. Climbers that are hardy annuals (HA) can be sown outside in early spring.

Cobaea scandens (cathedral bells) – HHA; large violet-blue bells.
Geranium 'Summer Showers' – HHA; pink and red.
Ipomoea (morning glory) 'Heavenly Blue' – HHA, sky blue.
Lathyrus (sweet pea) – HA; climbers; many colours.
Asarina erubescens – HHA; rose-pink trumpets; hairy leaves.

Thunbergia alata (black-eyed Susan) – HHA or HP; type form is orange, but mixed colours with black eye are now available.
Tropaeolum canariense (canary creeper) – HA; yellow flowers.

ANNUALS FOR THE ROCK GARDEN

Annuals are generally out of place in a rock garden unless they are very small. However, if carefully chosen they will provide colour at a season when few other plants are blooming. Those listed below may be sown direct or raised in boxes for transplanting. They are equally suitable for troughs, border edging and small beds.

Anchusa 'Blue Angel' – deep blue; compact and shade tolerant; 25 cm.
Iberis (candytuft) 'Fairy Mixed' – white, rose, purple, 20 cm.
Linaria 'Fairy Bouquet' – mixed colours; 22 cm.
Lobularia maritima: white, pink, violet; easy to grow; 20 cm.
Mesembryanthemum criniflorum (Livingstone daisy) – buff, apricot, crimson, pink; 8 cm; full sun.
Nemophila menziessii 'Baby Blue Eyes' – sky blue with white centres; 20 cm.

ANNUALS TO FOLLOW BULBS

By the time spring-flowering bulbs have finished blooming and their foliage has died down, it is becoming rather late to sow summer flowers – so plants already raised in punnets or boxes are often the best choice. The list of HALF-HARDY ANNUALS (pp. 17-18) gives ideas for suitable plants.

However, there are a number of colourful varieties that can be sown as late as mid-winter with success. Most of the ones listed under ANNUALS FOR THE ROCK GARDEN (p. 25) are suitable – but the following, which prefer sunny situations, are taller and may be preferred:

Dimorphotheca aurantiaca (star of the veldt) – white, yellow, salmon; daisy-like; 15 cm.
Eschscholzia – either single mixed or double art shades; 30 cm.
Phlox drummondii – mixed colours; 20-35 cm.

Right: Mixed tagetes in a border give a golden display to bring sunshine into a garden.

F1 HYBRIDS

Hybrid seeds have become very important in horticulture and will be increasingly so in the future. They are produced by breeding from two selected parents with special qualities, which are usually combined in the offspring. Seeds from the first cross are normally called F1 Hybrids.

The production of this seed is time-consuming and costly. Because further generations are very variable, and in some cases there is no germination at all, it is necessary to repeat the same cross year after year. The advantages are often considerable: quicker and more even germination, extra vigour producing higher yields, a greater resistance to pests and diseases, greatly increased periods of blooming, and larger flowers.

Many new strains of F1 petunias, *Begonia semperflorens*, ageratum and African marigolds are just a few of the flowering plants that have been transformed in recent years. Tomatoes, sweet corn, Brussels sprouts and cabbages are among the vegetables that have been greatly improved. But the most exciting of the recent introductions is the multiflora type of zonal geranium, which blooms from seed sixteen to twenty weeks after sowing. The 'Carefree' and 'Pinto' strains are available in separate colours, and are often on sale at garden centres from mid-summer onwards. Most home gardeners prefer to buy them as plants, as they need warm greenhouse temperatures (22° to 23°C) to germinate freely. These strains are very bushy, with at least two heads of bloom at the time of purchase.

Below: A colourful mixed border brightens up a front-garden path.

GROWING SWEET PEAS

Lathyrus odoratus is the plant we all know as the 'sweet pea', and it is among the most attractive, prolific and sweet-smelling of all the annuals.

There are clubs and societies entirely devoted to the cultivation of sweet peas – probably the only annual to have achieved such popularity. Since sweet peas were introduced into Britain from Sicily in 1699, the original small purple flower has been transformed into the wonderful range of large-flowered, multicoloured varieties available today. And there are now dwarf strains, suitable for small gardens, that do not need staking.

Those who grow for exhibition go to great lengths to achieve perfection, starting by digging a trench two spits (spade depths) deep and incorporating much well-rotted animal manure. Good results can be obtained with rather less effort – so long as a fertile, well-drained site in full sun is chosen, with plenty of humus in the form of compost or manure.

Provide support for the usual climbing types in the form of netting firmly fixed to uprights. For exhibition flowers with long stems, sweet peas are sometimes grown as cordons with side shoots removed, allowing just one or two stems to develop. Most growers, however, let their plants branch freely, after pinching out the main shoot at about 30 cm.

Although it is quite satisfactory to sow the seed direct into prepared soil outdoors in autumn or early spring, most people prefer to sow in trays or pots of potting mix. Peat pots are highly suitable, as the undisturbed root system may then be planted out intact.

The seeds sometimes have a hard coating. If so, either chip the coating with a sharp knife or soak the seeds in water for twenty-four hours before sowing.

Sweet peas are susceptible to fungus diseases in the soil, so it is advisable to plant in a different place each year. If this is not possible, it may be necessary to sterilise the soil with Basamid (which entails a delay of about six weeks before planting out).

Although sweet peas are usually grown in straight rows, like vegetables, they can also be grown in circular clusters, an informal type of planting that looks much better in a mixed border. Arrange 2-metre canes in a circle with a diameter of about 60 cm, encircle them with netting, plant your sweet peas about 20 cm apart around the netting, and in due course you should have a beautiful pillar of blooms.

Picking the faded blooms once a week will prolong flowering. When the plants have finished flowering, cut them off at ground level. As with other members of the pea and bean family, the roots grow nodules that have a high nitrogen content; if they are left to rot in the soil, they will therefore benefit the next crop.

You can obtain seeds for tall-growing sweet peas under various names and in separate colours; in most cases they will have at least five flowers on each stem. These are the best for general cultivation.

There are intermediate strains, such as 'Snooper', which has dark green foliage without tendrils or wavy flowers. Smaller still is the 'Bijou Dwarf' strain, which does not exceed 30 to 40 cm in height and has ruffled flowers with a rich colour mixture and stems long enough to pick.

Some distinctive sweet peas called 'Two Tone' have been bred. Each of the flowers is bicoloured, the standards being a different colour from the wings. They are best sown in early spring, as they are summer-flowering; and need to be planted in full sun, since they require eleven to twelve hours of daylight to flower. Their colours include combinations of rose, white, pink, lavender and navy.

To prolong vase life, pick sweet peas before they are fully open; singe the end of the stems in a flame or plunge them into boiling water briefly, then stand the blooms up to their necks in cold water.

Below: Mixed sweet peas (Lathyrus odoratus).

PERENNIALS

PERENNIALS IN THE GARDEN

A perennial plant is one that can be expected to reappear every spring and grow and flower during the summer, year after year, then die down in winter. A hardy plant is one that will withstand the winter cold and damp. Naturally this hardiness will vary according to regional climate. Some hardy perennials lose all foliage in winter, but others retain it in whole or in part.

Below: A colourful mixed border containing Californian poppies.

GARDEN BEDS

BEDS OR BORDERS

In days gone by, perennial plants were usually grown in long straight flowerbeds known as herbaceous borders. This formal arrangement invariably used a hedge or a wall, or possibly flowering shrubs, as background. And naturally the taller varieties of plants were grouped at the back, with shorter ones in front.

In recent years, however, the idea of island beds of informal shape has become a popular alternative. Normally grass will surround such beds, but when appropriate a pathway – curved where possible – can be used on one side. Many of the lower-growing perennials look most attractive if allowed to spill over the edge.

MIXED BORDERS

Some people now talk about 'cottage borders' and try to reproduce the informal style of planting associated with British country cottages.

In order to obtain a continuous display annuals and biennials feature prominently, often supplemented by a few shrubs and possibly some herbs. This style of gardening usually involves replanting the annuals much more frequently, but the result can be very charming and pleasurable.

ISLAND BEDS

One advantage of the island bed is that it is usually situated well away from trees, with the result that the plants are sturdier and require less staking than in a border next to a hedge or wall. In selecting the plants for an island bed, the height of the tallest should not exceed half the total depth of the border.

The tallest plants are arranged in the centre, with shorter ones in front of them and the shortest of all next to the verge. If you are planning to lay paving along the verge, set it so that the slabs are level with the lawn, to facilitate mowing and eliminate edge trimming. The paving will allow the front row of plants to spill over the edge in a very attractive manner.

Right: An island bed with plants arranged according to height.

GROUND PREPARATION

A

WEEDS

When preparing the site for a new bed or border it is important to eliminate perennial weeds. Docks, couch grass, bindweed and creeping thistle are all impossible to eradicate from a mixed perennial border, so must be eliminated first.

This could take some months, but with the aid of an all-purpose herbicide it is not impossible (weedkillers for driveways are not suitable). Annual weeds such as groundsel, chickweed and shepherd's purse matter much less, as they are more easily controlled by hoeing or mulching.

DRAINAGE AND SOILS

Some gardeners have the good fortune to have gardens with light alluvial soil, or even volcanic soils – while some have sandy or gravelly soils, and many others have heavy loam or clay.

Those in the last category must ensure that the border drains freely in times of heavy rain, otherwise some plants may not thrive. If the ground is on a slope it should shed rainwater easily, but on a level site drainage tiles may be required.

One cannot expect all plants to flourish in wet, sticky soils over the winter, especially as some soils tend to bake hard in summer sun. Although there are a few that will grow in wet soils, a bog garden is a more suitable place to grow them.

Sandy, gravelly or volcanic soils are invariably free-draining and likely to dry out in summer. They will respond to dressings of peat, compost and manure. A few perennials, such as lupins, do not thrive on alkaline soils; a test of the soil will indicate which species to avoid.

A neutral soil with a reading of pH6 is ideal; if the figure is much lower, then an application of lime is recommended after digging but before planting.

The site should be cultivated to a depth of 30 cm – if possible (A), without bringing up subsoil or clay. At the same time, add compost and manure. To lighten heavy clay soil, work in organic material such as spent hops, seaweed, shredded garden rubbish, poultry or animal manure, or peat or sand. A rotary hoe will do this admirably, but does not go deep enough to take the place of initial digging.

PLANNING

Undoubtedly the best results are obtained by planning your planting on graph paper (scale 1 cm to 1 metre), so that an assessment of the number of plants required and careful placement of them can be made.

An average density for planting is four or five plants per square metre, but this will vary between the small plants at the front and the larger ones further back. In choosing the plants personal likes and dislikes must be a first consideration; and length of flowering season is important in order to get maximum effect. Time of flowering should be considered so as to avoid periods without flowers, and plant heights are also of considerable importance. For the inexperienced, a good reference book is therefore essential.

The spire-like growths of delphiniums, verbascums, hollyhocks and the taller lilies should be intermingled with plants of a bushier nature; it is also necessary to place groups of late-flowering plants in front of early-flowering plants such as watsonias, iris, campanulas and spring bulbs, so that the gaps left after flowering are not too obvious. It is also possible to plan the best effect for a particular time of year – avoiding mid-summer, for example, if that is when you are usually away on holiday.

COLOUR

With so many factors to consider, the most important of all can easily be forgotten – and that is colour.

As you plan, you may want to put together colour groupings which you have observed with pleasure elsewhere. At the same time, you can avoid placing groups of the same colour and same flowering time close together; and the same applies to colours that you know will clash. If you have duly attended to all the other factors, the result will be a pleasing and harmonious picture, for nature does not often clash her colours.

A great many books are available on perennials that are suitable for gardens in the northern hemisphere, and in the main this information is an excellent guide for cool regions. But be aware of seasonal and calendar variations. In warm regions where frosts are light or non-existent there are a number of perennials that are unlikely to flower satisfactorily. This is not always appreciated by gardeners who have only had experience of cool conditions. Peonies are a notable example: with occasional exceptions, they seldom produces flowers in frost-free areas.

Other flowering plants that are unlikely to do well in most warm regions include aconitum, *Helleborus niger*, incarvillea, *Linum perenne*, lupins, oriental poppies, *Primula florindae* (although *Primula belodoxa* and most other primulas will flower satisfactorily), scabiosa, veronica, meconopsis and *Trollius eruopaeus* (though *Trollius ledebouri* flowers well).

On the other hand, in warmer areas one has the opportunity to grow other plants, many of which do not have hardy or half-hardy varieties. These include asclepias, bletilla orchids, marguerite daisies, clivia, dietes, eucomis, gloriosa, hippeastrum, isoplexis, *Ageratum houstanum*, vallota, veltheimia, euryops, tender impatiens and canna.

Right: Peony 'Jan van Laewen'.

SPACING

For the best effect you generally need to plant groups of three or more plants of each variety, though some that divide very easily (such as *Lobelia* 'Queen Victoria') can be planted in groups of five to ten, quite close together. If you are prepared to wait a year or two, using annuals and biennials to fill gaps in the meantime, many of the stronger perennials can be divided (see p. 46) in order to gradually fill the border fully.

However, with some perennials – for example, gypsophila, limoniums (statice), thalictrums and eryngiums – division is not possible. Others may be divided and replanted after growing for one full season: for example, Michaelmas (Easter) daisies, asters and helianthus (sunflowers).

MIXED BORDERS

In many cases gardeners prefer to use perennials in association with flowering shrubs – particularly camellias – often supplemented by bulbs.

But while the ever-popular cultivars of *Camellia japonica* prefer partial shade a large proportion of perennials grow best in full sun, so you need to choose perennials that tolerate shade. On the other hand, cultivars of *Camellia reticulata* and their hybrids, plus *Camellia sasanqua* cultivars and hybrids such as 'Donation' and 'Spring Festival', grow well in full sun and make highly suitable companions for perennials. There are, of course, a large number of other flowering shrubs that enjoy the sun. Your choice of shrubs to use with perennials will be influenced by their colour, height and flowering time.

You probably won't get it completely right first time, but most perennials can be moved quite safely in winter or early spring – so do not hesitate to experiment and learn from experience.

MAINTENANCE

Although less staking is usually required for borders in full sun that are away from trees, staking will be necessary in gardens that are exposed to wind. It can be extremely aggravating to admire a group of plants one day, only to find they are almost flat the next. Try as you might, it is then often impossible to tie them so that they look natural in manner.

Prevention is so much better than cure. The wise gardener will have a supply of small stakes in a convenient corner to put around the clumps in good time – before they collapse.

Twist ties and, sometimes, string will also be needed. Twigs pruned from trees and shrubs are often suitable, particularly those from bamboo, apple trees and some conifers. If evergreen prunings are used, they can be stowed away while the foliage dies off. For tall gladioli, eucomis and delphiniums a straight stake plus twist ties is all that is required (each main stem will require staking).

Another method is to stretch large mesh netting at a suitable height above the clump and let the stems grow through it.

Early in the season, before growth is much developed, weeds can be controlled by spraying with a weedkiller, so long as the spray nozzle is kept close to the soil and spraying is done on a still day.

Later, hoeing may be necessary and very likely some hand weeding. An annual dressing of fertiliser will encourage most plants to flower more freely. A general-purpose fertiliser (5% Nitrogen : 5% Pphosphorus : 5% potassium) is suitable and should be applied early in the spring.

Poultry manure makes an excellent low-cost spring mulch, applied at a depth of not more than 3 cm.

Summer maintenance should include removal of spent flowerheads, watering during dry spells, and mulching with fine organic material in order to prevent moisture from rapidly drying up.

In autumn or early winter, most of the top growth should be cut down and composted. Some summer-flowering plants, such as kniphofia (red-hot poker), aristia, dietes and some day lilies (hemerocallis), have evergreen foliage that will need to be trimmed.

If these plants are included in the border, they will add materially to the display in late summer and autumn.

The modern dahlia flowers very freely and is available in many shapes and sizes. Of chrysanthemums, the late-flowering Korean hybrids are probably the easiest for the non-specialist; they are available in single and double forms and a variety of colours. Seed strains are offered, which produce a mixed bag: about half will probably need to be discarded, the best being grown on for the future.

The great advantage of the 'Koreans' is their hardiness through the winter, and they require a minimum of spraying to keep them healthy. Nor is it necessary to disbud them, although some 'stopping' may be required early in the season.

Mulch dahlias and chrysanthemums well for good results.

Right: Dahlias

PERENNIAL FAVOURITES

MAXIMUM SUN ALL DAY ☀   SUN ✹   PARTIAL SHADE ○   SHADE ●

NAME	COLOURS	HEIGHT IN CM/M	SUN OR SHADE	FLOWERING TIME	REMARKS
Alchemilla mollis (lady's mantle)	yellow	30 cm	✹ ○	Spring	attractive foliage
Anchusa (morning glory)	brilliant blue	1 m	✹	Spring	short-lived
Anemone japonica (windflower)	white, pink	70 cm	✹ ○	Autumn	
Aquilegia vulgaris McKana hybrids	various	90 cm	✹ ○	Spring	long spurs
Aster (Michaelmas daisy)	white, pink, red, blue	60 cm to 1 m	✹ ○	Summer	very bushy
Campanula latifolia (bellflower)	lilac, blue, white, violet	30 cm to 1 m	✹ ○	Spring	
Coreopsis grandifolia	yellow	60 cm	✹	Late spring	single or double
Delphinium elatum Pacific hybrids	blue and white shades	1.5 m	✹	Summer	beware slugs
Dianthus (pinks, carnations)	various	10-50 cm	✹	Spring	they like lime
Erigeron (fleabane)	mauve, pink, violet	60 cm	✹	Spring	
Gaillardia (blanket flower)	yellow, red/yellow	60 cm	✹	Summer	
Helenium (coneflower)	yellow to red/brown	60 cm	✹	Spring/Summer	
Hosta (plantain lily)	mauve	30-90 cm	○	Spring/Summer	attractive foliage
Hemerocallis (day lily)	pink, maroon, yellow, orange	90 cm to 1.2 m	✹ ○	Spring/Summer	
Kniphofia (red-hot poker)	scarlet, orange, yellow cultivars	1-2 m	✹ ○	All year	
Lupinus polyphyllus (lupin)	various	60 cm to 1.2 m	✹	Spring	cool regions only
Nepeta faassenii (catmint)	mauve	30 cm	✹ ○	Spring/Summer	
Paeonia (peony)	white, pink, red	80 cm to 1 m	✹	Spring	cool regions only

| | | MAXIMUM SUN ALL DAY ✷   SUN ✹   PARTIAL SHADE ◯   SHADE ● | | | |
NAME	COLOURS	HEIGHT IN CM/M	SUN OR SHADE	FLOWERING TIME	REMARKS
Phlox	white, crimson, pink, scarlet	60 cm to 1 m	✹ ◯	Summer	not clay soils
Pyrethrum	white, pink, red	60-90 cm	✹	Spring	not clay soils
Rudbeckia (coneflower)	yellow	60 cm to 1.2 m	✹	Summer	single or double
Salvia x superba	violet purple	75 cm	✹ ◯	Spring/Summer	
Verbascum (mullein)	yellow, white, also coppery	1 to 1.5 m	✹	Spring/Summer	some are biennial

PERENNIALS FOR WET PLACES

The table on pp. 42-43 gives a selection of perennials that require wetter than average conditions. Gardeners lucky enough to be able to provide the necessary conditions can grow a number of beautiful plants that are not often seen. Modern water-irrigation systems will help in borderline cases.

Right: Lupins.

			MAXIMUM SUN ALL DAY ☀	SUN ☼	PARTIAL SHADE ○	SHADE ●	
NAME	COLOURS	HEIGHT IN CM/M	SUN OR SHADE			FLOWERING TIME	REMARKS
Astilbe (hybrids)	white, pink, red	60 cm	☼ ○			Spring	
Astilbe simplicifolia	pink spikes	1.2 m	☼ ○			Summer	
Aruncus sylvester (goat's beard)	creamy white plumes	1.75 m	○ ●			Summer	
Candelabra primulas:							
Primula helodoxa	yellow tiers	75 cm	○			Spring	sheltered
Primula florindae	yellow, orange, crimson	60 cm	○			Spring	sheltered
Primula pulverulenta							
Primula aurantiaca							
Filipendula rubra venusta	feathery pink	2 m	☼ ○			Summer	good foliage
Gunnera manicata	giant green leaves	2 m	☼ ○			Spring/Summer	large flower spikes
Hakonecloa macra 'Aureola'	yellow foliage	25 cm	☼ ○			Winter/Spring	a grass
Hosta (all species and cultivars)	green, variegated or mauve foliage	30 cm to 1.2 m	○ ●			Spring	attractive flower spikes
Iris laevigata	various	1 m	☼ ○			Spring	
Iris kaempferi	white, blue, lilac, violet	1.5 m	☼ ○			Spring/Summer	open, flat flowers
Lobelia fulgens 'Flamingo'	pink flower spikes	1 m	○			Late summer	
'Queen Victoria'	scarlet flower spikes	80 cm	○			Summer	
Lobelia syphilitica	blue flower spikes	80 cm	☼ ○			Summer	
Lobelia vedrariense	rich purple	1 m	☼ ○			Late summer	
Lythrum salicaria	rosy purple spikes	1.5 m	☼			Summer	vigorous
Mimulus lutea (monkey musk)	yellow, bronze, red	50 cm	☼ ○			Spring/Summer	spreading

		MAXIMUM SUN ALL DAY ☀	SUN ✹	PARTIAL SHADE ◯	SHADE ●	
NAME	COLOURS	HEIGHT IN CM/M	SUN OR SHADE		FLOWERING TIME	REMARKS
Onoclea sensibilis (sensitive fern)	spreading fern	50 cm	●		Spring	deciduous
Osmunda regalis (royal fern)	very large fronds	2 m	◯			deciduous
Rodgersia pinnata 'Superba'	pink spikes	1 m	◯		Summer	
Trollius europaeus (globe flower)	yellow	50 cm	✹		Spring	cool only
Trollius ledebouri	golden yellow	50 cm	✹		Spring	most regions

Right: Iris kaempferi 'Summer Storm' has deep purple petals.

PLANTS FOR SHADE

There can be considerable differences in the degree of shade required. In cool regions some of these plants almost prefer full sun, while in hotter regions the same plants prefer some degree of shade.

In the list below, plants indicated by an asterisk (*) prefer to be grown in the shade of trees, especially in the warmer and sunnier areas. Areas under trees tend to become extremely dry due to the tree roots – so an annual mulch of compost or poultry manure often works wonders.

Alstromeria pulchella	Heuchera
Aquilegia	Impatiens
Acanthus *	Iris foetidissima *
Arthropodium cirrhatum	Liriope muscari *
Anemone japonica	Meconopsis
Bergenia	Mertensia
Billbergia	Myosotidum *
Campanula persicifolia	Omphalodes
Campanula latifolia	Pachysandra
Clivia miniata *	Polygonatum *
Convallaria *	Polyanthus
(Lily of the Valley)	Primula
Dicentra	Platycodon
Digitalis	Rodgersia
Epimedium	Solidago
Gunnera	Thalictrum
Helleborus *	Trillium *
Hemerocallis	Tradescantia

PERENNIALS THAT NEED FREQUENT DIVISION

The following give their best results if divided and replanted every second or third season:

Aster novi–belgii	Helianthus
Aster novae–angliae	Lychnis viscaria
Anthemis	Monarda
Artemisia lactiflora	Oenothera fruticosa
Dianthus	Physostegia
Erigeron	Rudbeckia
Gaillardia	Sidalcea
Helenium	Solidago

SEED PROPAGATION

Some perennial species are still grown from seed, as species reproduce true from seed provided that there is no opportunity for cross-fertilisation. However, nowadays selections with improved characteristics – known as 'cultivars' – are numerous, and these have to be increased by vegetative means. In some cases, including cultivars of aquilegia, hollyhocks (*Alcea rosea*), delphiniums and geum, seedsmen have 'fixed' a number of strains by line breeding, as they breed true or very nearly true.

Seed should not be used when named cultivars are superior. To illustrate this point, take a look at aquilegias. The long-spurred McKana hybrids offer a lovely mixture of bright colours and large, elegant flowers. None of the individual colours would breed true; but there are several named cultivars which do, such as 'Crimson Star' (crimson and white) and 'Nora Barlow' (double pink and green). For other colours it is necessary to go back to the species – for example, *Aquilegia caerulea* (60 cm), with blue-and-white flowers, and *Aquilegia longissima* (70 cm), with glaucous leaves and yellow flowers that have spurs 10 cm long.

The single *Pyrethrum roseum* is another example. Seed strains of pink and red come sufficiently true to have superseded the old cultivars 'E.M. Robinson' and 'Harold Robinson', whereas the named doubles must be grown by division. Neither this plant nor cultivars of *Scabiosa caucasica* should be divided until growth has begun in spring, since for both these plants division in the autumn (especially in cool climates) can be fatal.

Left: Alcea rosea.

1

2

4

DIVISION

Many cultivars of perennial plants – such as *Aster novi-belgii,* helianthus, helenium, monarda and physostegia, to name just a few – may be increased quite easily by dividing the rootstock.

This is normally done in late winter to early spring. By that time many of the new growths will have begun a new root system; they may therefore be replanted outdoors or potted straight away. If more increase is required, you can take top cuttings when the shoots have reached 20 cm; the cuttings then need to be rooted under glass.

1 Some vigorous perennials develop into large clumps that require considerable physical effort to break them up. One can be faced with a solid clump of interlocking roots, perhaps 30 cm across. Driving two border forks, back to back and close together, into the clump is often the only way to make an impression. Hostas, hemerocallis (day lilies) and astilbe are examples.

2 In the case of plants like hostas it is also necessary to use a strong knife, cutting the crown vertically in order to separate the growth buds,

each with its share of the root system. During the first season each strong bud will develop into a plant; but the full beauty of foliage and flower will not develop until the second or third season.

3 Alstroemerias, on the other hand, should be divided and replanted when they are dormant at the end of summer. Even the cultivar 'Walter Fleming' can be safely handled at that time and will make new growth before the winter.

4 *Paeonia officinalis, Paeonia lactiflora* and *Paeonia lobata* – which are tough, hardy plants – should be divided in the autumn by cutting the roots with a sharp knife to leave either one, two or three eyes on each plant. They may then be replanted straight away. If you delay division beyond the autumn, that will mean less growth and fewer, if any, flowers. Once you have planted them, leave them undisturbed for up to ten years.

PROPAGATION FROM CUTTINGS

Perennials that form a woody rootstock are normally propagated from cuttings taken from the first flush of growth in spring, or subsequently as further suitable growths develop. The cuttings are struck in sand under close conditions, with or without bottom heat (A), after the application of hormone powder suitable for softwood cuttings. Anthemis, *Aster amellus*, gaura, lythrum, scrophularia and *Gypsophila* 'Rosy Veil' are examples. The more popular *Gypsophila* 'Flamingo' and *Gypsophila* 'Bristol Fairy' need ideal conditions for rooting; otherwise they have to be grafted.

Named cultivars of *Lupinus polyphyllus* and *Delphinium elatum* need special treatment. The roots should be lifted in early winter from open ground and planted in a cold frame, or a sheltered outdoor site in warm regions. As growth develops, the cuttings are removed when 7 cm long and with a solid heel. Often a second and possibly a third batch may be taken, after which the stock plants are discarded. Both these plants need to be rooted in cool conditions, with little or no artificial heat, and shaded if the sun is strong. Hormone powder will assist rooting.

Campanula persicifolia and some other campanulas make numerous small white shoots around the crowns of one-year-old plants. Lift the plants around mid-winter and use these small shoots – either with or without green leaves – as cuttings between 1.5 cm and 2.5 cm long. Dibble them into sandboxes 2.5 cm apart, with the tips at ground level. Usually all will root and, if planted out later in light soil, will make good clumps by autumn.

A

Left: Campanula pyramidalis.

GRAFTING GYPSOPHILAS

As already mentioned, *Gypsophila* 'Flamingo' and 'Bristol Fairy' are often grafted, in order to obtain a better 'take' than is possible when they are grown from cuttings.

Sow seed of *Gypsophila paniculata* in early spring and plant out in early summer to produce a batch of rootstocks. These are lifted in the winter with the root systems complete and, if need be, bedded outdoors. Roots of pencil thickness are cut up into 7 cm lengths (cut the tops square, but give the bases a sloping cut). When your stock plants of *Gypsophila* 'Bristol Fairy' and 'Flamingo' have begun growth, these sections of root are cleft in the centre and a wedge-shaped scion of the desired cultivar is inserted, with the cambium layers lined up on one side. The scion may be held in position in any way convenient, but good results can be obtained with no binding at all. The grafted roots are dibbled into sand in boxes or tubes and kept in close conditions; the advantage of using boxes or tubes is that the plants are more easily hardened off.

ROOT CUTTINGS

Many perennials can be propagated by means of root cuttings. The stock plants should be grown in the ground, rather than in planter bags, because thick cuttings root and shoot much better than thin cuttings. Generally they should be pencil thickness or thicker, except if the plants normally have thin roots.

The following are usually grown from root cuttings: *Anchusa italica, Catananche caerulea, Papaver orientale, Romneya coulteri* and verbascums. The following have thinner roots, but the same principles apply: *Anemone japonica, Phlox paniculata* and *Primula denticulata*. Phlox plants produced in this way are normally free from eelworm, which is a serious disease in some countries.

There are some tuberous plants that have numerous dormant eyes, such as *Acorus calamus, Liatris spicata*, tuberous irises, and zantedeschia. It is possible to propagate these by removing the eyes with part of the tuber, treating them with fungicide and striking them in a sterilised medium. With zantedeschia the fungicide treatment is especially important, as the corms rot easily after damage. The tubers should be in a dormant state at the time of treatment.

FOLIAGE CUTTINGS
Lachenalia pearsonii may be increased by cutting mature leaves horizontally into strips 8 cm wide, then treating the sections with hormone powder and setting them in sandboxes (with the lower edge in the sand) in a cool greenhouse. Small bulbs will form on this edge and in due course may be separately boxed. Blood lilies, such as *Haemanthus katherinae*, may be propagated the same way, inserting the leaf cuttings in sand in mid-summer.

MIST PROPAGATION
Only a few herbaceous perennials derive any benefit from mist propagation; and in the case of pelargoniums (all types) and silver-leaved plants, mist is positively harmful and leads to serious stem rot.

Regal-pelargonium stock plants should be cut back during late summer while the weather is warm and growth is active.

The new growth will provide excellent cuttings for rooting in frames or in a cool greenhouse and may be grown on for a good display the following spring.

PESTS AND DISEASES
Young succulent growth in the spring attracts slugs and snails. Snail pellets are an effective remedy and easy to apply.

Hostas and some campanulas are prone to damage by garden pests; it is especially necessary to watch hostas because they are grown mainly for their foliage, which can be perforated easily. Delphiniums often fail when tiny slugs eat the embryo shoots during winter. To keep the slugs off them, put an 8 cm mound of sharp sand or fine scoria over the whole crown when you cut away the old stems in the autumn. The new shoots should then be quite strong when they emerge.

Aphids can be troublesome. Spraying with any insecticide will control them to some degree, but a systemic insecticide will give more lasting control. Caterpillars, which usually appear in summer, are also best controlled with a systemic spray.

BULBS

BULB BASICS

1

2

3

4

The term 'bulb' is loosely used to cover a wide range of plants, including corms, tubers and rhizomes. All of them have storage organs beneath the ground in one form or another.

You can incorporate bulbs into your garden by naturalising them throughout a lawn or by including them as part of a herbaceous border, flowerbed or rockery. They can be grown successfully in many climates and soil conditions, and there are species suited to every region, no matter how harsh the climate. Spectacular results can be achieved by enriching the soil, feeding, and watering with care; but there are also many hardy varieties that manage to thrive in low-maintenance landscapes, with just a minimum of care and attention. Some multiply quickly year after year and can be lifted, divided and replanted to fill every corner of the garden.

TYPES OF BULBS

Bulbs can be divided into four main categories, differing in their structure beneath the ground as well as in their foliage and flower types.

1: BULBS

Bulbs (e.g. daffodils and tulips) are modified leaves that have become swollen food-storage scales. They have a basal disc, from which the roots emerge, and an oval or pear-shaped profile.

2: RHIZOMES

Rhizomes (e.g. canna lily) are stems that grow either at or just below ground level and spread horizontally. The foliage emerges from the top of these horizontal stems, while the root system develops underneath.

3: CORMS

Corms (e.g. gladioli) are modified stems. Most of them lack regular layers or scales, but have a protective outer skin and are solid inside, not layered like bulbs.

4: TUBERS

These are divided into two groups. Stem tubers (e.g. cyclamens and tuberous begonias) generally grow at ground level and are solid and fleshy; they have shoots emerging from the top, and roots going into the ground from the base. Root tubers (e.g. dahlias) grow below ground level and have shoots arising from a piece of stem at the crown.

Bulbs can be grown in conjunction with many other species. Some of the most spectacular displays are created when bulbs are overplanted with annuals, and the bulbs simply emerge through the young plants. The annuals can be timed to flower simultaneously with the bulbs, or to follow the bulbs so the garden bed has colour over a long period. In fact it is generally a good idea to follow bulbs with a planting of annuals, as the garden can look rather bare during the period when the bulbs' foliage is wilting after flowering.

The wilting foliage must never be cut back: it should be allowed to die back naturally, to provide a good storehouse of nutrients for the following season.

If you are thinking of growing bulbs beneath annuals, bear in mind that the demand for feeding will be quite high, since both the bulbs and the annuals will need sufficient nutrients for healthy, productive growth.

Below: Bulbs planted among other plants help to create a colourful display.

HEALTHY SOIL FOR BULBS

Bulbs require moderately rich and well-drained soil, and it is important to provide these growing conditions if you want to achieve good results. As bulbs contain a store of nutrients, they will usually flower well the first year even if planted in poor soil. In subsequent years, however, they will not flower well if the soil is poor.

For maximum flowering, the ground needs to be well prepared before planting. The most effective way of creating a good growing environment is to add plenty of organic soil-building materials in the form of manure and compost. As well as adding valuable nutrients to the soil, these soil builders will improve its texture, structure and drainage qualities.

Compost can be made using three bins: one in use; one decomposing; one being built.

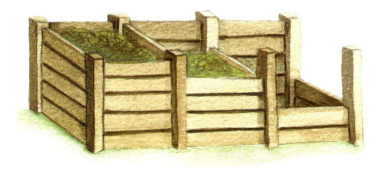

USEFUL SOIL ADDITIVES

COMPOST

It will pay you to produce a constant supply of home-made compost to add to garden beds as a mulch. Have three heaps going at once: one to use, one in the process of breaking down, and one being built. Mushroom compost adds texture to the soil, but lacks many basic nutrients.

MANURE

Cow, horse, sheep and poultry manures are the oldest and most accepted soil builders used in both agriculture and domestic landscaping. They improve soil texture and drainage, and provide a good supply of nutrients for plants. Never use fresh manure: always allow it to rot well, otherwise sensitive plants may be damaged.

SEAWEED

Gardeners living near the sea have the advantage of being able to bring home seaweed to add to the garden. Rinse the salt away thoroughly, chop up the seaweed, and either add it to your compost heap or use it directly in the ground.

HOW TO MAKE COMPOST

Home-made compost is a valuable soil additive and one that is easy to prepare, even in a small garden. Where ground space is limited, invest in a compost bin or tumbler that can be stored in a corner out of the way.

Compost is made by combining a range of organic materials and ensuring that they have both moisture and air circulation to hasten decomposition. Well-made compost will generally be ready for spreading on the garden after eight to twelve weeks. During this time tremendous heat will have generated inside the heap, reducing the organic materials into light, friable humus (soil).

When using a compost tumbler, the turning action aerates the compost and hastens decomposition. However, it is essential to add water regularly, to keep the process going.

A compost heap made on the ground needs to be turned regularly with a fork so air can penetrate. It should also be watered weekly in order to maintain the breaking-down process.

Suitable ingredients for a healthy compost heap include leaves, grass clippings, straw, kitchen scraps, shredded bark, manures and wood ashes.

Below: A rotating drum for compost.

PLANTING AND PROPAGATING BULBS

When choosing bulbs for the garden, always look for the healthiest and strongest specimens. Obviously this is impossible when buying by mail order; however, the majority of mail-order nurseries are reputable and only send out their best and healthiest stock.

Always look at bulbs, corms and tubers closely, and choose firm ones that seem solid and heavy for their size. With bulbs and corms, the larger and heavier they are the better in terms of flowering potential.

When selecting tubers, simply look for healthy specimens, since size is not so important. Check the outer skin carefully and choose those with the least damage.

Do not buy bulbs that are obviously shrivelled or have any soft spots, particularly around the base or the neck. Reject bulbs with any sign of mould, no matter how slight, and look carefully to ensure there are no insects that could weaken or destroy them.

PLANTING TIPS

Bulbs generally survive and flower well the first year, even when poorly planted. They can even survive being planted upside down, although this is not recommended! As already mentioned, the soil should be enriched with plenty of organic matter prior to planting; but there is no need to incorporate specific fertiliser into the planting holes, as the bulbs' own store of nutrients will see them through the first flowering season. Subsequently they will require annual fertilising in order to maintain the best results.

1 Generally bulbs need to be planted at twice their own depth (i.e. a bulb 2 cm tall needs to be planted at a depth of 4 cm). If soil drainage is poor, some sand in the base of the planting hole will create a better growing environment.

2 A close look at the bulb will determine which way up to plant it. Generally the base is flatter than the top, which has a slight point. With the more rounded bulbs, it can be hard to tell unless there is some evidence of a shoot.

3 Excavate a hole, allowing sufficient depth for sand if it is required.

4 Position a plant marker or slender stick in the hole beside the bulb or bulbs. This may save you from accidentally digging them up later.

5 Position the bulb or bulbs in the hole. Remember that planting three or more bulbs together creates a better, clumped effect.

6 Replace soil around the bulb, pressing down firmly to ensure that there are no air pockets, but taking care not to apply too much pressure.

7 Avoid overwatering. Bulbs are susceptible to fungal disease and will rot in the ground if too much moisture surrounds them.

BULB PROPAGATION

Most bulbs, corms and tubers can be propagated easily, by lifting and dividing them every few years. In fact most will benefit from being divided occasionally, as flower production is reduced if they are left undisturbed indefinitely.

BULBS

The way in which bulbs are propagated depends on their structure. True bulbs produce small offsets, which grow around the base of the mature bulb. These in turn will grow into mature bulbs once they have been separated from the parent bulb.

Use a fork to lift the bulbs, and gently break off the small bulbs. Sometimes they fall off naturally when lifted.

The immature bulbs should be replanted in a special area of the garden, where they will follow their normal growth cycle for two years until ready to flower and transplanted back into the main garden.

CORMS

Corms produce cormlets around the edge of the base of the mature corm every season. In order to propagate, lift the corms and gently pull away the cormlets; then replant the mature corm. There may be evidence of a previous corm that has withered and died: this should be pulled off and discarded. The cormlets can be grown for one season in a separate bed, then transplanted into the garden when they are ready to flower.

RHIZOMES AND TUBERS

Rhizomes and tubers are propagated by cutting the mature stock with a clean, sharp knife. For it to be able to grow, make sure that each cut section has either an eye or a section of stem. Replant immediately where the plant is to grow.

HOW TO PROPAGATE POPULAR BULBS

NARCISSUS

Daffodils and jonquils should be lifted every three or four years. Wait until all the foliage has completely died down; then lift with care, using a spade or fork. The mother bulb will be surrounded by small bulbs, which should break away without any problems. Store them in a cool, dark place for replanting in the autumn.

DAHLIAS

During late autumn, as the dahlias' foliage begins to brown, lift them for storing and replanting the following spring. This should be done every year. Use a clean, sharp knife to cut the tubers, making sure that each has a section of the crown and at least one dormant eye.

IRISES

Irises and similar rhizomes need to be divided every three years, or they will show signs of overcrowding. In autumn, use a fork to lift out the root mass, then cut off the rhizomes growing on the outer edge with a sharp, clean knife. To compensate for reducing the root mass, cut back the foliage to about half its size. Replant immediately.

LILIES

Lift the bulbs every three years and remove the old stems. Carefully separate the bulbs, including the small bulblets and offsets. Replant immediately.

GLADIOLI

Gladiolus corms should be lifted every few years. If several corms have formed, they can be separated; or if there is just one large corm, it can be cut in half and the two halves replanted. When cutting corms, always use a clean, sharp knife.

TUBEROUS BEGONIAS

Begonia tubers need to be cut when new shoots appear on them. Use a clean knife and cut down through the tuber, making sure each section has an eye. Place the tubers to dry for a few days in a cool, dark, dry place before replanting.

TULIPS

Tulips will not continue to flower year after year unless they are lifted and stored in a cool, dry place until autumn, when they should be planted in the spot where they are to grow. Tulips produce offsets, in the same way as daffodils; these can be replanted into a separate bed and left undisturbed for a few seasons until they are ready to flower.

GENERAL MAINTENANCE

MULCHING

Mulching the soil on top of bulbs will not prevent them from emerging and helps to reduce garden maintenance in many ways.

1. – MULCHING STOPS WEEDS FROM EMERGING.

2. – MULCHING KEEPS THE SOIL MOIST BETWEEN WATERINGS AND PREVENTS THE SURFACE FROM DRYING OUT.

3. – MULCH IMPROVES SOIL TEXTURE BY KEEPING IT LIGHTLY MOIST.

4. – WHEN ORGANIC MULCH IS USED, A STEADY STREAM OF VALUABLE NUTRIENTS IS SUPPLIED TO PLANT ROOTS.

5. – AS THE MULCH BREAKS DOWN, IT BUILDS THE SOIL INTO RICH, FRIABLE HUMUS.

1 With bulbs, the best time to mulch is after initial planting and then again when the first shoots appear.

2 A good layer of manure mulch applied once the bulbs have died back will help to feed them the following season.

The best mulches are compost, animal manures, bark chips, and leaves or leaf mulch.

WEEDING

Bulbs do not easily compete with weeds, which deplete the soil of moisture and nutrients. If the area around the bulbs is well mulched, weeding will be less of a problem. If, however, weeds persist, water the ground several hours before weeding. This is less traumatic for the bulbs and makes the task easier: if the soil is lightly moistened, weeds should lift out easily.

Avoid heavy cultivation, which will disturb bulb growth and possibly damage new shoots.

WATERING

Although regular moisture is required for healthy growth, bulbs should not be overwatered. Provided the soil has good drainage qualities, overwatering should not be a problem. However, if the soil is inclined to be boggy, attempt to improve the texture by adding plenty of compost or manure. The amount of watering the garden requires depends on the type of

1

2

soil, the style of garden, and the general climate and amount of rainfall.

WHEN TO WATER

During warm or hot weather it is best to water either early in the morning or early in the evening. Wait until direct sun has moved from the garden before turning your sprinkler on. In cold climates, if watering is needed during the winter, choose mid-morning rather than late afternoon, to avoid the risk of overnight cold freezing water trapped on the foliage, which can damage certain species.

FEEDING

The bulbous part of the plant – whether rhizome, tuber, corm or bulb – is its nutrient storehouse. When you buy bulbs, they normally contain a store of nutrients that is sufficient for the first year's growth. For good results, consider the following:

ENRICHING THE SOIL

Always incorporate plenty of rich organic matter into the ground before planting your bulb stock. This also helps to improve drainage and supplies additional nutrients to the growing plants. If the soil is rich, no extra fertiliser should be required during the first growing season.

AVOIDING NITROGEN-RICH FERTILISERS

Too much nitrogen will encourage rapid foliage growth, often at the expense of flower production. So avoid poultry manure, and use horse or cow manure as a soil builder.

MULCHING

After the bulbs' foliage has died down, mulch the ground thoroughly with a mixture of compost and well-rotted manures.

BULB FOOD

There are several brands of specially formulated bulb food that give excellent results. These can be used as a top dressing during the period when the foliage is dying down, then applied again early in the growing season when the flowers are forming.

LIQUID FERTILISER

Make sure the liquid formula is balanced and not too rich in nitrogen. Apply a weak solution once a fortnight during the main growing period.

AN ALPHABET OF BULBS

AGAPANTHUS (AFRICAN LILY)

A native of South Africa, this plant forms a clump of deep-green strap-like leaves, from which emerge tall stalks topped by circular flowerheads. Relatively hardy, they thrive in any fertile well-drained soil; choose a sunny sheltered position, especially in cooler climates. Miniature forms are available. Colours range from white to various shades of mauve and blue. Propagate by dividing the clumps, or from seed.

ALLIUM (ORNAMENTAL VARIETIES)

A delightful bulb for the cottage garden, with tall slender stems and dramatic flowerheads. Quite easy to grow, allium species like moderately rich well-drained soil and should be positioned in full sun. Plant bulbs in late autumn or spring, and mulch with well-rotted animal manure to produce good foliage and flowers. Each year the bulbs can be lifted and divided in the autumn. The healthiest bulbs can then be replanted to form new clumps.

AMARYLLIS BELLADONNA
(NAKED LADY, BELLADONNA LILY)

A native of South Africa, each stem of this beautiful bulb has a profusion of trumpet-shaped rose-red flowers that bloom from the summer through into autumn. For repeated good displays season after season, plant in full sun in deep rich soil, ensuring that the position is sheltered. They look spectacular as a border along a driveway, or against a warm sunny wall.

ANEMONE (WINDFLOWER)

Anemones require rich well-drained and slightly moist (not wet) soil; they will only thrive if the right growing conditions are provided. For spring flowering, plant in early winter, provided that the ground is not too cold. A warm sheltered position will give good results.

Below: Agapanthus, a handsome bulb that is easy to grow in most soils and conditions.

BABANIA (BABOON FLOWER)

A native of South Africa, babania is a member of the iris family; it has strap-like foliage and funnel-shaped flowers. There are many hybrids, with colours ranging from white through yellow, cream, red and mauve. For good results, plant corms in full sun in moderately rich well-drained soil. It is suitable for indoor pot cultivation in cool regions.

BEGONIA

Begonias have marvellous foliage and attractive, sometimes showy, flowers. Begonias need soil that is rich in organic matter and a warm, sheltered, semi-shaded position. Regular watering is required in summer, especially when the plants are flower-ing – but take care not to waterlog the soil and in winter keep the soil rather dry (this applies to both potted and garden begonias).

BRODIAEA X TUBERGENII

Native to the Americas, these delicate bulbs look best when planted in dense groups. Their flowers range through various blues to purple, and some are tinged with orange. Relatively hardy, they are able to survive in any average garden that provides a well-drained sunny position, preferably with the protection of a south-facing wall. Allow them to

multiply year after year; once established, they require very little attention. They are suitable for greenhouse cultivation in cold regions.

CANNA (INDIAN SHOT)

Canna lilies form green, brown or purple foliage with tall spikes of elegant flowers in the orange, red and yellow colour range. Enrich the soil with plenty of organic matter before planting out in a sunny sheltered position in early summer. Bring the plants under cover before autumn frosts begin.

CARDIOCRINUM GIGANTEUM (GIANT LILY)

This lily can reach a height of more than 2 metres. It has heart-shaped foliage and tall stems of droop-ing white trumpet flowers in summer. The right growing conditions are vital: soil must be rich and moist, and good drainage is important. Water freely in dry weather, and mulch with well-rotted manure or compost every spring. Being monocarpic, the plants die after flowering, leaving offset bulbs to reach flowering size after three to five years.

CHIONODOXA (GLORY OF THE SNOW)

These charming small bulbs start flowering in late winter and continue through to mid-spring. They are best positioned in full sun or semi-shade, and look effective when scattered in drifts beneath deciduous trees. Add organic matter to the soil before planting, and ensure adequate drainage. Cultivate by lifting and separating the bulbs.

COLCHICUM (AUTUMN CROCUS)

Providing a dramatic burst of colour in autumn, colchicums grow to 30 cm in height and emerge without foliage. Select a sunny or semi-shaded sheltered position, and ensure that the soil is rich and moist before planting in late summer. Autumn crocuses are ideal as part of a rock garden or as border plants. To divide, lift and move the bulbs while in flower; replant immediately.

CRINUM (CAPE LILY)

There are more than a hundred species of these large showy bulbs, with fragrant flowers in the rose, pink and white colour range. Choose a sunny sheltered position, and ensure the soil is rich and well drained. Water well, especially during the summer. Only lift every four years; propagate by gently removing offsets from mature bulbs.

CROCUS

Small, hardy bulbs that are natives of Europe and Asia Minor, crocuses look delightful naturalised in drifts beneath deciduous trees, or as part of a rock garden. They can be grown in a wide range of soils and conditions. Choose a sunny position and water well, but avoid overwatering as they should not be waterlogged. Propagate by removing and replanting offsets.

CYCLAMEN

Cyclamens have attractive leaves and slender stems with soft flowers in the pink, red and white colour range. They need a warm sheltered environment, with soil that is rich in humus and well drained. Water well, especially in summer, but take care not to overwater. Only use fertiliser sparingly.

Below: Crocuses grow well in pots.

DAHLIA

These long-established favourites have dramatic flowers in a variety of forms, many of them large and colourful. They can be grown in a wide range of soils and conditions. Large varieties need staking to prevent damage when the flowers emerge.

ENDYMION (BLUEBELL)

Very easy to grow in a wide range of soils and conditions, bluebells should be positioned in a location where they cannot dominate or smother other species. They look effective naturalised beneath deciduous trees, and are useful for shady places where little else will grow. Plant in moderately rich well-drained soil. Clumps can be lifted and divided after the foliage dies down.

ERANTHIS (WINTER ACONITE)

A low-growing tuber, which spreads like a ground cover, with flowers of vivid yellow. Although hard to establish, once they find a suitable environment they should thrive, provided that the soil is rich and moist. Water regularly, especially during warm summer weather. The tubers produce offsets that can be used for propagation; before planting, soak them in water overnight.

ERYTHRONIUM

A member of the lily family, erythronium has a variety of foliage and flower forms. It thrives in moderately rich well-drained soil in semi-shaded situations. The corms should be planted in autumn and normally require little maintenance apart from watering in summer. Clumps can be divided every three or four years to produce new plants.

FREESIA

One of the most prized garden bulbs, freesias are available in many flower colours and forms, including some excellent new giant hybrids, which are very showy indeed. Valued for their glorious scent, freesias require full sun and a sheltered site, with light, rich, sandy, well-drained soil.

FRITILLARIA

Crown imperials have tall stems topped with spiky leaves and drooping bell-like flowers. Requirements vary according to the species – although in general the soil must be moist but well drained, and a sunny but sheltered position must be found. Some species need to be left undisturbed for a minimum period. When dividing, ensure that the bulbs are replanted immediately, as they dry out rapidly.

GALANTHUS (SNOWDROP)

Snowdrops have deep-green foliage and slender stems topped by delicate white pendulous flowers. Flowering in late winter and early spring, they require deep, rich, moist soil and either full sun or semi-shade in order to produce a good display. Bulbs can be lifted and divided every few years.

GALTONIA CANDICANS (SUMMER HYACINTH)

A summer-flowering bulb with fragrant white bell-like flowers on a tall, slender stem, Galtonia needs an open sunny position, with protection from strong winds, and a moist well-drained soil. Plant bulbs in clumps of three or five, and mulch well with organic matter during winter. Propagate every four years by separating the offsets from the bulbs towards late summer.

GLADIOLUS (SWORD LILY)

The corms produce tall dramatic flower spikes and sword-like foliage. There are many hybrid forms, ranging from miniature to giant varieties, in a wide range of colours from creamy white through pink, salmon, orange and violet-blue to deep scarlet. Gladioli like a sunny aspect and well-drained soil enriched with plenty of organic matter.

GLORIOSA (GLORY LILY, CLIMBING LILY)

This spectacular climbing lily has flame-like red-and-yellow petals that turn to orange and claret as the flower matures. An unusual, exotic plant, it needs greenhouse cultivation except in the mildest and most sheltered areas, where it may be planted out in early summer for late-summer flowering. It climbs on tendrils and can be trained on a trellis or wall. A warm wind-protected site is essential.

HEMEROCALLIS (DAY LILY)

This bulb produces a dense clump of slender leaves and tall stalks of dramatic flowers that can be orange, yellow, lavender, purple, red, maroon, bronze, pink, cream, or off-white in colour. A well-drained soil enriched with organic matter will give the best results. Divide in autumn when clumps become crowded, usually after three to six years.

Left: Hemerocallis (day lily) has tall slender stems and showy flowers.

HIPPEASTRUM (AMARYLLIS)

A native of South America, hippeastrum produces strap-like leaves and tall stems that grow to about 1 metre in the right conditions. These carry three or four showy trumpet-shaped flowers that can be multi-coloured, red, orange, pink or white. Rich, moist soil and good drainage are essential for success. Except in warm countries, it requires indoor or greenhouse cultivation.

Below: Ipheion forms a carpet of star-like flowers.

HYACINTHUS (HYACINTH)

An extremely popular group of bulbs, originally from the Mediterranean, hyacinths are valued for their scent as well as their attractive blooms. The colour of the waxy bell-shaped flowers, borne in late winter or in the spring, range from white, through blue and purple, to red, pink, salmon, buff, yellow and pale cream. Some of the larger species reach 45 cm in height.

Forced potted bulbs can be planted out during the spring to recover and continue flowering. Left undisturbed, they will flower year after year.

With hyacinths, good drainage is essential for success. For the best effect, they should be planted in clumps or en masse.

IPHEION (TRITELEIA, SPRING STAR FLOWER)

Either blue or white tinged with blue, ipheion's delightful star-like scented flowers are borne in spring or early summer. Growing to a height of 20 cm, it will thrive in sun or partial shade and prefers moderately rich well-drained soil. Clumps should be left undisturbed for several years, until they are well established.

IRIS

There are many species and varieties of iris – in two forms, rhizome and true bulb. They can be seen in flower over most of the year, depending on the variety and time of planting. Colours cover the entire spectrum, except for true red; there are also many multicoloured varieties. All irises thrive in full sun, in soil that has good drainage and that has been well enriched with organic matter.

IXIA (AFRICAN CORN LILY)

A native of South Africa, this warm-climate corm can survive in a sunny position outdoors in mild regions or be grown indoors in pots. It thrives in rich well-drained soil in sunny rock gardens. The colours range from dark red, through pink, orange and yellow, to cream, white and green.

LACHENALIA (CAPE COWSLIP)

This South African lily has thick stems and delightful tubular flowers in the red, orange and yellow colour range. The flowering time is late winter to early spring. After the foliage has turned yellow it should be cut back, then the ground mulched with well-rotted compost. It prefers an open sunny position. In cool regions it needs to be grown in a greenhouse or potted indoors.

LEUCOJUM (SNOWFLAKE)

A charming bulb for late winter, not to be confused with snowdrop (*Galanthus*). The foliage is deep green and strap-like, while the small white bellflowers are tipped with green. Growing to a height of 45 cm, snowflakes thrive in moderately rich free-draining soil and can be planted in either full sun or semi-shade.

Below: A majestic purple-and-yellow iris.

LILIUM (LILY)

You can choose from the many hundreds of lily varieties – which range in height from 30 cm to 2.5 metres and are available in a wide spectrum of colours, from pure white, through cream and yellow, to pink, orange, red, maroon, lilac and purple. The hardiness of lilies varies according to variety, so ask the nursery or plant supplier to confirm this at the time of purchase. In general they will thrive if planted in full sun or semi-shade, in deep, rich, well-drained soil.

Below: Daffodils are the most popular and widely grown bulbs.

MUSCARI (GRAPE HYACINTH)

The dense heads of rich-blue fragrant flowers make these bulbs ideal for planting in borders and edges. Easy to cultivate in a wide range of soils and conditions, grape hyacinths need to be planted in full sun, as shade will increase leaf growth and reduce the quantity of flowers.

NARCISSUS (DAFFODIL, JONQUIL)

The most widely grown garden bulb, narcissus is available in dozens of flower types, colours and forms. Ranging in height from 8 cm to 45 cm, both jonquils and daffodils can be grown with great success in a wide range of soils and conditions. However, their most important requirement is good drainage. Before planting, enrich the soil with plenty of organic matter – or if planting them at the base of trees, lightly mulch with well-rotted manure to improve the soil conditions.

Popular types of narcissus include:

TRUMPET DAFFODILS:
Large corona segment. One flower per stem.

LARGE-CUPPED DAFFODILS:
Shorter corona. One flower per stem.

SMALL-CUPPED DAFFODILS:

Corona only one-third of the size of outer petals.
One flower per stem.

DOUBLE DAFFODILS:

Multiple corona segments, fluffy appearance.
One flower per stem.

TRIANDRUS HYBRIDS:

Medium-size corona. Several flowers to each stem.

CYCLAMINEUS HYBRIDS:

Petals curved backwards. One flower per stem.

NERINE (SPIDER LILY)

A tall-growing bulb with slender stems topped in
autumn by eight or more tubular flowers that have
a graceful spidery appearance. The flowers range
in colour from white to pink, orange and red,
according to species. With the exception of *Nerine
bowdenii*, these require greenhouse cultivation in
cooler regions. Bulbs exposed on the soil surface
must be protected from frost. Avoid lifting nerines
for several years. Instead, leave them to form a
large established clump.

PRIMULA VULGARIS ELATIOR (POLYANTHUS)

Although chiefly grown outdoors, polyanthuses are
also suitable for pot culture. Flowers up to 4 cm
across are carried in large trusses on stout stems
above the leaves. For good results, plant in an
open sunny position in rich, moist soil. Offsets can
be replanted the following season.

PUSCHKINIA SCILLOÏDES (STRIPED SQUILL)

A spring-flowering bulb with dainty pale-blue or
white star-like flowers, striped with darker blue on
each petal. For the best results a cool climate is
preferred, with rich, moist soil and good drainage.
Leave the bulbs undisturbed for several years until
flowering diminishes, at which point they should
be lifted and separated.

RANUNCULUS

These spring-flowering tuberous-rooted plants produce tall stems of semi-double or double flowers,
ranging from red, through yellow and orange, to
cream, white, pink and multicolours. They require
plenty of water during the growing period, but it is
important to let the soil dry out after the foliage
has died back. Many gardeners dig up the roots at
this stage and store them in a cool, dark, dry place
until planting time the following season.

SCILLA (SQUILL)

This is a cool-climate bulb that flowers in late winter and early spring. Scillas have strap-like foliage and stems of bellflowers that can be blue, violet, lilac, pink or white. Plant in full sun or semi-shade in deep, rich, well-drained soil. Mulch well after the foliage has died down.

SPARAXIS (HARLEQUIN FLOWER)

A half-hardy corm that is easy to grow, sparaxis produces brightly coloured red, yellow, orange, pink, purple or white flowers in late spring. In mild regions it can be planted in autumn in rich well-drained soil in a sheltered position. Clumps can be left undisturbed for years. To propagate, lift the plant so you can detach the cormlets and replant them; they will take two seasons to flower. Sparaxis is also suited to potting.

SPREKELIA FORMOSISSIMA (JACOBEAN LILY)

A summer-flowering bulb, with strap-like foliage and dramatic deep-red flowers resembling orchids. In cold regions it needs to be treated as a cool-greenhouse plant. In mild frost-free districts it can be planted in autumn in a sunny position in good well-drained soil. Water regularly, and feed as the foliage begins to emerge. Bulbs can be left in the ground for several years until flower production declines; then lift, separate and replant in the autumn. Wait until foliage dies back before lifting.

STERNBERGIA

Sternbergias develop very quickly, being planted in mid-summer to produce blooms in mid-autumn. The bright-yellow flowers are borne on short stems and are similar in appearance to crocuses. Each bulb produces just one flower.

After flowering has finished the foliage continues to grow, eventually dying back in the spring. Do not cut back the foliage, but allow the cycle to be completed naturally.

TULIPA (TULIP)

Magnificent cold-climate bulbs with numerous flower forms and colours to choose from, tulips range in height from 15 cm to nearly 1 metre. They can be grown in full sun or partial shade and need rich, moist soil with good drainage. Sandy soil, which is slightly alkaline, suits them perfectly.

When the foliage turns yellow and starts to wither, the bulbs may be lifted for storage. Small offsets can be set on one side and replanted the next season; these may take two seasons before starting to flower.

WATSONIA (BUGLE LILY)

These showy plants with strap-like leaves and tall flower spikes can be used to make a splendid high border or grown in clumps in a wild or cottage garden. They thrive in warm climates in deep rich soil with adequate drainage; in cooler regions they are suitable for indoor cultivation in pots.

Some varieties grow to as much as 2 metres when established. Flower colours include lavender, salmon, pink, orange, red and white.

ZANTEDESCHIA (ARUM LILY)

Zantedeschia corms develop tall stems with elegant spathes, and some varieties have arrow-shaped or heart-shaped leaves. The spathes may be white, yellow, green-and-white, pale pink or wine red. In a mild climate moist well-drained soil is essential; plants can be grown beside streams or waterways with great success. Add plenty of organic matter to the soil prior to planting, then feed with a liquid fertiliser in early spring as the spathes develop. Well-established clumps can be divided in autumn.

In cooler regions arums are best suited to tender greenhouse cultivation in pots, but can be placed outdoors during the summer. Some varieties are suited to hardy aquatic cultivation; these are able to survive winter conditions in most regions.

Below: Tulips are well suited to cold climates and require rich, moist, well-drained soil.

ROSES

ROSE TYPES

Cherished by many gardeners, roses have stood the test of time: they are still among the most popular garden plants and have come to symbolise numerous events.

Fossilised roses found in Europe, Japan and America are reputed to be 35 million years old. The first pictorial evidence we have is a six-petalled flower in a fresco unearthed at Knossos in Crete, dating from 1500 BC, which has been heavily restored.

For my own part, when I began my career as a gardener I was not particularly fond of roses – but as I became familiar with them my interest steadily increased.

Below: A delightful mixed display, featuring 'The Fairy', 'Angelina' and 'Silver Jubilee'.

Many plants are remarkable for their beautiful flowers, shape and perfume, but very often the flowering period is limited. In one way this is an advantage, since we look forward to the time when they are in bloom, just as we look forward to the different seasons. But roses have the merit of producing delightful flowers in abundance over a long period, year after year.

Whether for ornamental display in the garden or for picking, they have few rivals – but many people shy away from growing roses, assuming that they will have to implement major spraying and fertiliser programmes in order to achieve good results. However, rose bushes are in fact extremely hardy plants, capable of surviving almost total neglect; and with a little care and attention, even unpromising specimens will grow into strong, healthy-looking bushes with attractive blooms.

Roses fall into the following main groups: hybrid teas, floribundas, ramblers and climbers, shrubs and miniatures. Except for ramblers, climbers and standard roses, these groups are usually referred to as bush roses.

HYBRID TEAS

Hybrid teas flower singly or in small clusters; often there is only one flower per stem. For this reason they are preferred by some gardeners, as the blooms look very attractive as cut flowers. Two of my favourite hybrid teas are 'Fragrant cloud'® and 'Rosenthal'. These are very fragrant red roses that look superb in an elegant vase – a must for the table when guests are expected.

FLORIBUNDAS

Floribundas have many flowers on one stem. Because of this cluster-flowering they are highly suitable for mass planting and are sometimes used as hedges. One floribunda that looks excellent as a hedge, or when planted en masse, is the extremely healthy forever-flowering 'Iceberg'®. Another popular floribunda that blooms particularly well is the recently introduced 'Sexy Rexy'®.

Recently some floribundas have been greatly improved through breeding with hybrid teas. The bushes are more vigorous, the individual flowers larger, and the clusters more open with fewer flowers. These improved floribundas are sometimes advertised as grandifloras.

Left: 'Fragrant Cloud', a beautiful hybrid tea.

Left: 'Masquerade', a popular floribunda.

RAMBLERS

Although these are climbing roses, because they are lax and tractable they can also be grown horizontally. They can be trained along low fences or allowed to sprawl over the ground, ending up as ground cover.

The main difference between climbers and ramblers is that the growth of climbers is stiffer and more erect, whereas ramblers are lax. One of the best-known ramblers and a favourite of mine is 'Albertine'. This is a vigorous free-flowering rose that looks effective on low or high fences, trellises and pergolas.

Below: 'Albertine'.

CLIMBERS

Climbing roses are often used to cover walls, fences and pergolas, and can make an extremely attractive feature.

They have numerous leaders, and by tying and pruning them you can encourage laterals to branch off and produce blooms. The more vigorous climbers cover as much as 5 to 6 metres, while the shorter types – sometimes known as pillar roses – have a 2-metre spread.

In a situation where a vigorous climber is flowering freely on an overhead pergola, a pillar rose can be planted beside the pillar support to give a fuller flowering effect lower down.

SHRUB ROSES

This group covers an exceptionally wide range of modern hybrids derived from the species (the species being wild roses). It includes all the older types of garden roses, which are often referred to as 'old-fashioned' roses.

Old-fashioned roses have shown an appreciable resurgence in recent years, and no wonder. They are naturally almost disease-free and have a wonderful charm of their own. Their history is fascinating, their petal form extremely varied, and many of them have an exquisite perfume.

Their names alone are intriguing:

'Cardinal de Richelieu'

'Duchesse de Montebello'

'Félicité Parmentier'

'Frau Dagmar Hastrupp'

'Honorine de Brabant'

'La Reine Victoria'

'Souvenir de la Malmaison'

'Souvenir d'un Ami'.

These are just some of the names that immediately conjure up visions of the grand old gardens spread throughout western Europe.

In fact it was Napoleon's wife, the Empress Josephine, who helped bring the rose to the forefront among popular garden plants. Early in the nineteenth century she assembled in her garden at Malmaison, near Paris, one of the largest collections of roses, including wild species and garden forms with hybrids. From there, old-fashioned roses were developed further, eventually leading to the modern-day rose.

MINIATURES

A miniature, as the name suggests, is a very small rose, often no higher than 10 cm when planted. Miniatures can be planted in a bed amongst other rose bushes, or treated individually or as a low border plant. They can also be grown in pots or window boxes, or even in rockeries.

Miniature roses budded onto standard rootstocks are known as standard miniature roses. These are fast gaining favour. Two miniature weeping standards I like are 'Snow Carpet'® and 'The Fairy'. Planted in clay pots, they make attractive plants for a courtyard or patio.

Below: 'The Fairy', a miniature standard.

CHOOSING THE RIGHT ROSES

A

B

First of all, you need to decide where you are going to plant your roses and whether you have any specific requirements. For example, do you want a mass planting of roses, a mixed bed, or climbing roses to cover a bare wall?

There are many choices and combinations that blend in very successfully, but avoid growing shorter roses behind taller ones, planting rose bushes too closely together or trying to grow them in totally unsuitable conditions.

Below: Standard roses planted in a mixed border.

JUST ROSES

If you have a very large garden, separate beds containing the same variety of rose (a minimum of nine to eighteen plants) will look extremely attractive. These beds can be square with nine plants (A), or rectangular with eighteen (B). Rectangular beds with a taller variety planted down the middle and lower varieties on either side can also be very effective.

Larger plantings of roses will be highlighted if the plants are evenly spaced and surrounded by a beautifully kept expanse of green lawn. Even one large rose bed looks exquisite in a sea of green.

In a small garden a long, narrow bed can be filled with bush roses, interplanted with standard roses towards the back. Standard roses give height at the rear of the planting, while bush roses give bulk and support to the stock onto which the standard roses are budded.

Weeping standards and miniature weeping standards on their own can look good – but rows of standards as an edging to a pathway or driveway, without any other vegetation, look stark and unimaginative.

MIXED PLANTING

Some bush roses look good combined with perennial plants. In a terraced garden three, five or seven roses, spaced about 75 to 90 cm apart, together with plants such as nicotiana, lavender or alyssum, may be particularly effective.

Cottage gardens are now very popular and can look extremely attractive. If space permits, old-fashioned roses make an ideal backdrop to one of these gardens. An edging of lavender (*Lavandula stoechas*) or English box, then a show of annuals and perennials, with old-fashioned roses or weeping standards or a combination of them further back, make a perfect setting for a sunny summer's day.

CLIMBING ROSES

Climbers can be used for many situations: on a fence as a background to a rose bed, covering archways, growing up through dead or living trees, or against buildings.

When selecting a climber, be sure it is the type you require. Some have beautiful blooms but only flower part of the season. Choose varieties that are repeat-flowering, unless you are keen to have a particular variety that does not repeat. Two healthy, vigorous and repeat-flowering climbers are 'Compassion' and 'Dublin Bay'®.

Below:
R. banksiae 'Lutea'.

POSITION AND SOIL

SUNSHINE

Roses are happiest in a sunny position. The less shade the better.

I have often observed roses planted under trees or being choked by neighbouring plants. Roses under trees look pitiful. Not only is there a lack of sunshine, but the rose's roots get very dry as they compete for moisture with tree roots that have invaded the rose's root zone.

AIR CIRCULATION

Roses like good air circulation but dislike draughts. Shelter them from strong winds, and avoid draughty or static air conditions.

DRAINAGE

Roses will not thrive in poorly drained soil. They dislike being waterlogged for any length of time.

SOIL

Roses will grow in any type of soil, provided it has been prepared correctly. They grow best in soils with a pH of between 5.8 and 6.5.

Once the roses are established, the aftercare of the soil plays a vital role in their health and vigour.

Left: Roses thrive in a sunny position.

PREPARATION FOR PLANTING

ADDING DRAINAGE

If drainage is a major problem in the area you have chosen for your new rose bed, then a drainage system will be needed to remove excess water.

A channel dug below the level of the rose bed, leading away from the area, is a simple solution. Place clay field pipes or perforated plastic pipes in the channel, then cover them with 2 cm of drainage chips (metal chips) to a depth of about 15 cm. To reduce costs, you can exclude the pipes and use drainage chips only, as water will filter through the chips and follow the natural drainage path.

If there is no suitable outflow for a drain, dig a deep soak pit at the channel outlet. Fill this with rocks and/or drainage chips. The water will slowly drain from this sump.

Another solution to drainage problems is to slightly raise the level of the rose bed. Water will run off to the lowest edges and eventually drain away.

SOIL PREPARATION

Soil rich in humus (decomposed organic matter) is excellent for most plants, including roses. If possible, prepare the soil some months before planting, to allow sufficient time for the organic matter to break down and for the soil to settle. Autumn is a good time to do this.

In new residential areas the topsoil is often removed during construction. Consequently the new residents inherit a clay soil that is hard and stony, or sandy if near the coast. The quickest solution is to remove the poor soil to a depth of 45 cm and replace it with good-quality topsoil.

In a garden that has 15 cm of good topsoil and very heavy clay underneath, dig out the turf for the rose bed area (and keep it); then remove the clay to a depth of 45 cm and replace it with topsoil.

An alternative method is to incorporate organic matter into the clay subsoil. With a spade, remove turf along the length of the proposed rose bed, then repeat this so that there are two spade widths removed. This will give you room to work. Next, dig over the clay subsoil, breaking it down with the spade. With a border fork, mix plenty of organic matter (to a depth of 10 cm) into the clay. You can use either mushroom compost, well-rotted compost from refuse bins, sheep or cow manure, pea straw, ordinary straw, or some soil conditioner from a local garden centre. Finally, dig out another row of turf and turn it upside down on top of the newly laid organic matter.

If you have not prepared a rose bed in advance, for immediate planting prepare the soil as described above and give it a good 'heeling over'. That is, after mixing in the compost, tread systematically all over the bed with the heels of your boots; then rake it over. This will ensure that the newly dug bed does not settle down at a later date. Do not heel over the bed when the soil is very wet – since valuable air pockets will be lost and the soil texture will suffer, creating a pudgy soil.

ADDING NUTRIENTS

Once the bed has been dug over, give it a light dressing of lime or dolomite in order to reduce soil acidity.

Although roses like the soil to be slightly acid, both new soil and old exhausted garden soil will benefit from such an application. Soil that is fairly acidic binds the necessary nutrients; by reducing soil acidity, dolomite and lime make these nutrients readily available. Whereas ordinary lime is calcium carbonate, dolomite is calcium magnesium carbonate – which is more beneficial, since it adds magnesium to the soil and therefore helps maintain an appropriate balance between levels of magnesium and calcium. Gently fork the dolomite or lime into the top 10 cm of the soil in the bed.

Prior to planting the roses, apply a light dressing of blood and bone to the soil, with superphosphate if desired. Personally, I prefer to feed my roses about a month after planting. I feel they need time to adjust to their new environment; after that they are able to make full use of nutrients that leach down to the root zone.

RECEIVING NEW ROSES

After buying new rose bushes in winter from a garden centre, or if they have been delivered to you by courier or mail, make sure the roots are kept moist at all times. Allowing the roots to dry out is a major cause of losses. Roses should therefore be planted as soon as possible after receiving them or taking them back home.

Growers dig out rose bushes to meet orders for late autumn. Although potted stock is convenient, bare-rooted specimens make it easier to inspect the root stock. Often they are packed in sawdust or with wet shredded paper around the root zone. After a while the roots dry out, so if you do not intend to plant your roses straight away, remove the packing and heel them into a vacant plot. Just dig a trench, place the rose bushes in it, then cover the roots with soil and heel them in.

SPACING

When planting rose bushes in a large bed, it is essential to mark out the future position of each with a small stake or bamboo stick. Otherwise, if the spacing is uneven, you will have to dig them out and start again. For vigorous bush roses, one pace from the bush's centre is ample space.

AVERAGE SPACING	
MINIATURES	30 CM
LOW COMPACT BUSH ROSES	45 CM
AVERAGE-SIZED ROSES	75 CM
VIGOROUS VARIETIES	1 M
CLIMBERS	3 M
(allow more for very vigorous climbers)	
STANDARDS	MINIMUM 1.2 M

PRUNING NEW ROSES

Contrary to popular belief, new rose bushes have not usually been pruned by nurserymen – only trimmed for ease of handling, packing and transport and for general appearance at the point of sale.

Often a rose grower will zoom along rows of 'ready to be sold' roses with an electric cutter, so that all the branches are trimmed to the same height.

BEFORE PLANTING ROSES

1 Remove all thin, spindly branches and any soft immature shoots, to retain a framework of strong, healthy branches.

1 (before planting)

2

1 (planting day)

2

3

4

2 Bush roses should be pruned back to approximately 13 cm from the crown (see page 00). Where possible, leave about three or four buds on each branch.

3 Make your pruning cuts just above strong a bud, preferably one pointing outwards. When pruning a bush rose, keep in mind the eventual overall shape of the trained plant: the centre of the plant will be a void, to encourage air circulation and sunlight.

4 Climbing roses should be pruned back to a height of approximately 30 cm; and standard roses to between 15 and 20 cm from the crown. Thin out surplus shoots, and shorten stems to the first good bud from the top.

PLANTING DAY

Roses can be planted during suitable weather at almost any time of the year, depending on whether the new plant is bare-rooted or potted.

From late autumn onwards, through the winter until the spring, is the most usual time. If the soil is fairly dry and the sun is out, then that is a good day to plant.

1 Keep the rose roots wet at all times. Once removed from their heeled-in position, soak the roots in a bucket of water.

2 If roots are damaged, split or partially broken, cut them back to where the root is intact.

The majority of rose varieties are budded onto multiflora rootstock (*R. multiflora* being a strong and vigorous old briar rose). Rose growers prefer to use this method, rather than taking cuttings, as the former produces a far greater and faster yield with a stronger root system.

The point where the rootstock meets the budded variety is known as the budhead, crown or union.

When you are planting a new rose, you need to bear in mind climatic severity and future spring mulching. In warm regions the budhead should show just above the surface of the soil, to allow for future mulching adding to the soil level. In cool regions, to avoid the risk of frost damage, set the crown just below the surface of the soil – but when mulching in future make sure the surface is even, since a depression will gather water and this is likely to seep down to the rootstock, causing rot.

This raises a further consideration when buying roses. Try to choose rose bushes that have been budded fairly close to the roots – no more than 15 cm above the root zone. If a rose has been budded higher than this, in order to plant it with the bud union just above ground level, the roots will have to be buried to a greater depth, where they may not receive water and nutrients as efficiently as when the roots are closer to the surface.

3 Dig a round hole in the rose bed, with a small mound in the centre to support the root system. The hole size should suit the root system and the height of the budhead. Place the roots on the mound to check if the depth of the hole is correct. Never curl the roots to fit the hole; if the roots are too long, prune them back as described above.

4 A small stake laid across the hole will help you to determine if the budhead is above or below the soil surface. Once the roots of the rose are sitting at the correct height, splay them evenly around the mound. Then begin to cover them, working fine soil between and over the roots and firming it down as you go.

STANDARDS

5 Standard roses are planted in a similar way to bush roses – but, to avoid accidental damage to the root system, drive a supporting stake firmly into the ground before planting.

6 After planting, use soft bands of sack webbing or old stockings to tie the rose's stems firmly to the stake, so that there will not be any rubbing when the wind blows.

I wrap the webbing twice around the stake (in order to prevent chafing the stem) and then wrap it around the stem twice.

7 Secure the webbing with two or three small flat-head nails driven through the webbing into the wooden stake, or by threading strong twine through holes in the webbing and tying it around the stake.

CLIMBERS

8 Climbers are planted in a similar manner to bush roses. Position them a minimum of 10 cm from any wall or pergola support, so that they lean slightly towards the support when planted.

This will make it easier to train the direction of new leaders than if the plant is placed hard against its support.

6

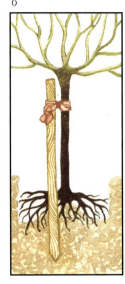

8

PRUNING

A

EQUIPMENT

Secateurs with 'parrot-beak' blades are needed, and loppers for cutting thick old branches. A pruning saw is sometimes needed to deal with larger branches, and to remove stubs or branches close to the budhead that loppers and secateurs are unable to reach. Gardening gloves are also needed to protect your hands.

Right: A good pair of secateurs and gardening gloves are essential when pruning roses.

BUSH ROSES

In mild areas pruning can be done in autumn or early spring. In areas subject to hard frosts the final pruning is best left until early spring, to avoid frost damage to tender young growth.

If modern bush roses are not pruned, they become straggly and diseased, carry a lot of dead wood, and ultimately regress. They will also produce fewer blooms.

An analogy I like to use is that if we allow our hair to grow too long it eventually develops split ends and grows less vigorously. A good trim every so often improves the shape and stimulates growth. Rose bushes are similar: an annual winter prune during the dormant period helps to rejuvenate them. Pruning assists natural methods of replacing old, unproductive stems with new and vigorous ones. Each summer, if well fed, most bush roses will develop new canes from the budhead.

DEAD AND OLD WOOD

The first items to remove from your bush are all dead wood, any weak or straggly branches, and – as far as is practical – old

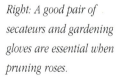

canes that are carrying only thin shoots. You should aim to retain a minimum of three to five canes on an established rose bush (A) – so always cast an eye over the whole bush before pruning and do not cut out all the old wood if there is no new wood to replace it.

When removing old or dead canes, make your cuts as close as possible to the budhead. You may need to scrape back soil or mulch to saw off the canes flush with the budhead. Any cane stub left on the budhead will be a potential harbour for disease.

REMOVING CENTRAL WOOD

Remove canes that are going to grow across the centre of the bush, ones that are too close to others, and stems that are crossing (B). Crossing canes inevitably rub against each other, causing scars that may weaken and snap, allowing infection to enter the plant.

The reason for removing central wood, or as much as is feasible, is to maintain an open bush that allows light to penetrate and air to circulate – and also to persuade new stems to grow outwards, away from the centre of the bush.

Incidentally, at first new stems are often reddish brown; only later do they have smooth healthy-looking green bark. When the stems are four or five years old, they tend to turn greyish brown, with the bark texture becoming rough and lined.

CUTTING BACK

Think of the ideal pruned rose bush as an open vase shape, with a minimum of five healthy young canes pruned so that they have buds facing outwards approximately 23 cm above the the ground (C). This is the ideal picture. However, roses seldom grow by the book!

Once you have removed all unwanted wood, you need to reduce the new canes to about 23 cm above the ground.

Close inspection of a healthy rose stem will reveal little buds appearing around the stem at regular intervals from its base, and under each bud a horizontal line called the leaf scar. These dormant buds, sometimes known as eyes or shoots, are the points above which cuts are made.

B

C

Below: A good cut.

Once you have selected a suitable outward-facing bud (seldom do all canes have buds facing outwards at the desired height), make a cut about 5 mm above the bud, sloping downwards away from the bud at a 45-degree angle. A cut made in this way helps water to run off the cut cane, taking it away from the bud, where it could cause damage.

Below: 'Blue moon', a hybrid tea.

PRUNING BASAL SHOOTS

Basal shoots – or 'water shoots' as they are often called because of their soft, lush growth (A) – are usually not hard enough to prune back during early summer. Nor do they have buds low down on their stems.

In cold climates they are best removed, because they are regularly damaged by frost. But in warmer regions, try to keep these water shoots – as they are the best wood on the bush for the future.

Treat the flowerhead (1), which is a cluster on short stems, as if deadheading: that is, cut the flower stem back to the first strong bud.

These canes will harden up and mature during the following summer, so that they are suitable for normal pruning during the following winter.

HYBRID TEAS AND FLORIBUNDAS

The general rule is to prune mature hybrid teas moderately, to approximately 23 cm from the ground, but to prune floribundas a little higher.

STANDARD ROSES

Standard roses do not have the same power of regeneration as bush roses, so do not remove so much growth when pruning. However, the principle is the same: prune to outward-facing buds, wherever possible, and try to keep the centre of the bush fairly open.

MINIATURES

Give miniature roses a light trim all over.

CLIMBERS

The aim is to replace as many of the old canes as possible with new ones (B).

As a rule, on the remaining old canes prune back the side shoots (the laterals growing off the leaders) to the second bud out from the cane (1). On the new canes, reduce the growing tip (2) – which will encourage them to become stronger and produce laterals on which flowers will bloom. The old and new canes should be spread out evenly along the support.

Climbing roses will flower much better if trained horizontally, as they then flower all along the branches, instead of just at the tips. Tie new growth to the support structure and, where necessary, renew old ties. Cut-up old stockings make excellent ties for climbers.

R. banksiae 'Lutea' is a popular yellow climber that flowers in early spring. As soon as this climber has flowered, it needs to be lightly pruned back. If it is pruned in mid-winter, then very few flowers will bloom the following summer.

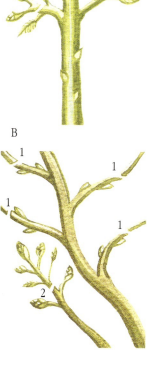

Left: 'Dorothy Perkins'.

RAMBLERS

True ramblers bloom only on wood grown during the previous year. In mid-summer, as soon as flowering has finished remove all old canes. This gives the new shoots better growing conditions for the remainder of the season. After removing the old canes, tie in the new ones.

We always used to prune our 'Albertine' rambler with hedge clippers. We would first remove only canes that had lost their vigour, then tie all the new canes into the pergola supports and check the ties on existing canes. After replacing the ties on the pergola frame, we would clip all the laterals with the hedge clippers. This is far quicker for a vigorous well-established rambler like 'Albertine': a quick removal of dead wood amongst the jumble of laterals and the job is complete.

OLD-FASHIONED ROSES

Many of the roses in this category – such as the alba, centifolia, gallica, damask and moss roses – need little pruning.

After flowering, very old wood should be removed in order to encourage strong young basal growth. These growths may be shortened by a third in mid-summer to avoid wind damage.

Apart from removing dead and spindly wood, which is essential, you can prune old-fashioned roses to suit your own needs. The ones that I have at home are 1.5 metres high and 1 metre wide.

EXCEPTIONS

Some bush roses produce most blooms if you prune them lightly, instead of using traditional hard pruning methods to produce an open vase shape. Many of these roses flower well on pencil-sized pieces of growth – among them 'Iceberg'®, which is capable of flowering on a larger framework of wood, as it is a particularly vigorous and healthy variety.

'ICEBERG' ®

Remove any dead wood and spindly growth, then prune back all remaining growth to strong buds. As a general guide, the retained wood should be the size of a pencil.

A bed of nine vigorous 'Iceberg'® roses at the Lady Norwood Rose Gardens in Wellington, New

Zealand, used to reach a height of approximately 2.5 metres every summer. Each July I would take hedge clippers, together with a little garden stool for elevation, to clip this bed of roses into shape, down to a height of about 1.5 metres. Then armed with secateurs, I would prune out all the dead and spindly wood and modify any cuts made by the clippers that were too high above a bud.

For a well-established individual plant, or for a hedge or bed of 'Iceberg'® roses, this method gives a good shape and is rapid and convenient.

'FIRST LOVE'

This bush rose does not produce many basal shoots (see p. 88), so needs only a light pruning. I prune it using the vase-shape system, but retain several pencil-sized growths off mature canes if new growth is non-existent.

OTHER BUSH ROSES

Some roses, such as 'Josephine Bruce', 'Percy Thrower' and 'Europeana'®, have a spreading type of growth, often requiring that canes be pruned to an upward-facing bud so as to arrest excessive spread.

SUCKERS

Roses sometimes produce suckers from their multiflora rootstock. If allowed to grow, the suckers will eventually dominate the bush. Suckers are easily identified, as they have feathery leaflets of a lighter, dull green.

Pull or cut off the sucker with a sliver of rootstock. Don't cut it off above the growth point, or it will continue to shoot.

Below: 'Iceberg'.

CULTURAL CARE

When you have finished pruning, smear all the pruning cuts on major canes with a pruning paste or vaseline; even rubbing dirt into cuts will help seal the wounds. This will prevent fungus spores infecting the rose, since a fresh cut is an ideal entry point for infection. One fatal disease that can afflict roses is silverleaf.

Pick up all dead leaves and pruning debris from the rose bed. Do not compost these, either burn them or take them to a refuse tip. They contain overwintering spores, which if left in the rose bed will infect the roses in the spring.

SPRAYING PROGRAMME

For a top display of roses, a regular spray programme is essential. Having said that, many people spray irregularly or prefer to use organic sprays and still achieve good results. Irregular or non-existent spraying is noticeable towards the end of summer, when diseases such as rust appear and the rose bush may lose many of its leaves.

During very warm weather, especially in humid climates, mildew problems can be quite prevalent.

COMBINATION SPRAYS

There are combination sprays available containing several ingredients that control most pests and diseases. Some are supplied in powder form, some as a liquid. There are also chemicals suited to mixing in a water solution for spraying, but always check that they are compatible.

Many different sprays contain identical ingredients without the customer realising it. To further complicate matters, although each chemical has a common name, it may be sold under a dozen trade names, depending on who markets the product. Always read the labels on products: it is surprising how much useful information they provide.

There are many, many types of spray available for roses. Only the main groups are listed here.

WINTER SPRAYING

After pruning, spray rose plants and beds with a good clean-up winter spray.

I usually spray mine with lime sulphur. Winter rate: 1 part lime sulphur to 15 parts water. It controls powdery mildew, black spot, rust, moss, lichen and scale insects.

Another winter spray is made by combining copper oxychloride with all-purpose oil (not winter oil). Winter rate: 25 gm copper oxychloride plus 200 ml all-purpose oil, in 5 litres of water. The copper oxychloride controls black spot and downy mildew, while the oil controls rust, scale insects and red mite.

To mix the spray, half-fill the sprayer with clean water. Put copper-oxychloride powder into a measuring jug and fill it up with water. Stir the mixture thoroughly, then pour it into the sprayer. Rinse the jug with water and pour the residue into the sprayer. Pour the all-purpose oil into the jug, then fill it up with water. Pour the mixture into the sprayer. Rinse the jug and pour the residue into the sprayer. Then pour the rest of the water into the sprayer.

Always mix powder and liquid chemicals this way.

Some rose lovers prefer to spray their roses with lime sulphur before pruning, and then spray with a combination of copper oxychloride and all-purpose oil after pruning.

Note: Do not spray with all-purpose oil within fourteen days of using lime sulphur. These winter-application rates are designed for dormant deciduous growth only. Applying them to new growth would burn the buds and leaves.

EARLY SPRING SPRAYING

Once roses start to break into leaf growth insect problems are not so apparent, but you still need to keep fungal diseases such as black spot or downy mildew at bay.

In order to control these diseases, in early spring spray fortnightly with 25 mg copper oxychloride mixed with 5 litres of water. Some gardeners add 100 ml of all-purpose oil (the spring rate) to the copper oxychloride solution.

Note: Be careful with oil sprays in the spring, as the soft new growth can be damaged by these sprays. I have had good control in early spring with just the copper oxychloride spray.

SUMMER SPRAY PROGRAMME

After the last spring spraying, wait for two weeks then commence the main season's spray programme.

From late spring to late autumn, spray fortnightly. The main spray I used for ten years at the Lady Norwood Rose Gardens combined the following four ingredients with 5 litres of water:

1: DITHANE

Common name maneb (powder). Contact fungicide. Controls black spot and rust to a degree. Rate: 10 gm (approximately 4 level teaspoons).

2: BENLATE

Common name benomyl (powder). A systemic fungicide with protectant and eradicant properties. Controls powdery mildew and black spot. This is an excellent fungicide. Rate: 25 gm.

3: ALL-PURPOSE OIL

Common names sun spray, conqueror oil (liquid). Controls rust, red mite and scale insects, and helps smother aphids. Also acts as a wetting agent, which helps other chemicals stick to the plant. Rate: 50 ml.

4: MALDISON

Common name malathion (liquid). Can also be purchased as a powder. A contact insecticide. Controls aphids, mealy bugs, thrips, leaf-hoppers, caterpillars and beetles. At the Lady Norwood Rose Gardens, I only included malathion if aphids were present on the rose bushes. Rate: 10-15 ml (2-3 teaspoons).

Note: Use combination sprays on the day when you mix them. They will lose their effectiveness if they are left to stand for days in the sprayer.

SOME READY-MADE SPRAYS ARE:

1: SHIELD

Also known as saprene (liquid). A combination spray for roses and ornamentals. Controls black spot, powdery mildew, aphids and caterpillars, and to some degree rust. This spray is very popular with home gardeners as it is easy to use and quite effective. There is some doubt whether it controls rust adequately. Rate: 2 ml/5 litres water.

2: ROSE-AND-ORNAMENTAL SPRAY (POWDER)

Excellent combination sprays are made in powder form. They control black spot, rust, leaf-hoppers, beetles, mealy bugs and powdery mildew. Spray fortnightly. Rate: 130 gm/5 litres water.

3: GENERAL GARDEN SPRAY (POWDER)

You may want to use a general garden spray on your roses if you already have it at home. Controls beetles, leaf-hoppers, caterpillars, mealy bugs, thrips, powdery mildew, aphids and mite species. Spray fortnightly. Rate: 40 gm/5 litres water.

4: ROSE SPRAY (LIQUID)

Good liquid combination rose sprays are available. They control mites, aphids, woolly aphids, thrips, black spot, rust, and downy and powdery mildews.

If your roses are suffering from a fungal disease such as rust, one excellent spray to use on its own is:

5: CALIRUS

This systemic fungicide is both a protectant and eradicant. It is not compatible with other sprays. Spray fortnightly. Rate: 10 gm/5 litres water.

GENERAL CONSIDERATIONS

It is worth remembering that it is better to spray regularly to prevent diseases, rather than having to cure them.

Also, bear in mind that with your main summer spray programme it is advisable to alternate the types of chemicals used, since resistance to particular chemicals by plant varieties can develop.

To avoid resistance building up, it is as well to consider the use of alternative remedies or solutions, such as derris, dimethoate, dinocap, formothion, nicotine, tar oil, thiram and zineb.

SAFETY WITH CHEMICALS

1: ALWAYS READ THE LABEL AND INSTRUCTIONS BEFORE USING CHEMICALS.

2: SOME CHEMICALS ARE NOT COMPATIBLE WITH OTHERS. ALWAYS FOLLOW THE MANUFACTURER'S RECOMMENDATIONS.

3: USE CLEAN EQUIPMENT AND CLEAN IT THOROUGHLY AFTER USE. AVOID USING EQUIPMENT THAT HAS BEEN USED FOR APPLYING HERBICIDES.

4: DO NOT SPRAY WHEN THE FOLIAGE IS DEWY OR WET, OR IN STRONG WINDS.

5: NEVER EAT, DRINK OR SMOKE WHEN HANDLING CHEMICALS OR EQUIPMENT.

6: WASH YOUR HANDS THOROUGHLY WITH SOAP AND WATER AFTER SPRAYING. IF ANY CHEMICAL SPLASHES ONTO YOUR SKIN, WASH IT OFF WITH COLD WATER WITHOUT DELAY.

7: KEEP CHEMICALS AND SPRAY EQUIPMENT IN A SEPARATE LOCKED CUPBOARD WHEN NOT IN USE.

8: DESTROY EMPTY SPRAY CONTAINERS.

Below: A well-mulched rose garden.

CULTIVATION AND MULCHING

Winter is an excellent time to weed and gently fork over your rose beds – as it is easier to move amongst the bushes when there is no new growth, which can easily be broken off.

Gentle forking reduces soil compaction created while pruning and allows aeration of the earth. Do not fork too deeply, since well-established roses have a multitude of fine feeder roots lying just below surface of the soil.

Once cultivation is completed, cover the rose beds with a suitable mulch. An ideal one is mushroom compost (spent compost that has been used for growing mushrooms). This medium usually has a pH of 6.5, exactly as required by roses. Cover the beds to a minimum depth of between 5 and 7.5 cm to make it worthwhile, and do not be overconcerned about covering the crowns of the rose bushes.

BENEFITS OF MULCHING:

1: Mulching reduces weeding. The weeds that do come through are easily pulled out.

2: It keeps the soil at an even temperature during winter or summer. Roses thrive with a cool root run in the summer months.

3: It helps the soil retain moisture. When the soil is irrigated during the drier months, the mulch holds the moisture and helps prevent evaporation.

4: It greatly improves soil conditions. With clay soils, it improves texture, structure, drainage and aeration. With sandy soils, it improves their ability to retain nutrients and moisture.

5: It provides the plants with trace elements.

6: It encourages more feeder roots to develop, so the rose bush will produce more basal shoots each growing season.

MULCHES FOR ROSES
Mushroom mulch is a sterilised medium, so should not result in your rose garden inheriting weeds or diseases.

The gardeners of the Lady Norwood Rose Gardens were once offered some free stable manure. Delighted, we spread truckloads of the stuff on all the beds.

Several weeks later thousands of dock seedlings appeared. We had no option but to remove all the stable manure, then two gardeners very carefully weeded out all the dock seedlings. Mulches are meant to reduce labour – but on that occasion we increased it. So beware!

Some rose growers use untreated sawdust, straw or grass clippings as mulches. These are satisfactory, but they do initially deplete soil of some nitrogen and are not aesthetically attractive.

Below: Healthy blooms, 'Blessings'.

FERTILISING

Once the leaves on your rose bushes
are growing well it is time to feed them:
as the weather turns warmer, the feeder
roots begin to grow. When using fertiliser,
a little often is a good rule of thumb.

ROSE FERTILISER MIXTURE:

3 parts blood and bone

2 parts superphosphate

1 part sulphate of potash

1 part sulphate of magnesium

1 part sulphate of iron

Apply two handfuls of this mixture around
the drip line (not against the bush) at the
onset of spring. The should be followed
by a further application two months later,
and a third application (without blood
and bone) two months after that. After
each application, gently hoe the fertiliser
mixture into the mulch or soil.

If you do not want to go to the trouble
of making up your own mixture, you can
buy one of the ready-made rose fertilisers.
Most of these have nutrients and propor-
tions similar to the mixture given above.

If you make up your own mixture for the
third application, towards autumn, it is
important to omit the blood and bone.
At that time you need to slow down the
growth of your roses – but still need to
apply fertiliser, as the sulphate of potash
helps to harden the soft new wood that
the bush or climber has produced. It can
be frustrating to try to prune a vigorous
young cane in winter only to find that it is
still quite soft and therefore splits.

WATERING

Roses respond noticeably to irrigation in
dry months. A proper watering soaks the
soil, allowing the water to penetrate the
mulch and sink well down into the root
zone. As a general guide, during dry spells
use a sprinkler to cover the whole rose
bed for 30 to 45 minutes. Water your roses
this way every third day, or about twice
a week. Early morning or evening is the
ideal time, as water can make the blooms
fade, particularly in bright sunshine.

You will find that plenty of water helps
your rose bushes to throw up new canes.
One year I recall not watering the roses

for about two weeks at the peak of summer. Consequently the bushes started to look a little straggly – but after two good doses of water they perked up considerably and their foliage once again looked fresh and glossy. However, even more important, the usual abundance of new wood began to appear.

You will know when the roses have had enough water. Avoid overwatering, as that may leach nutrients from the soil.

DEADHEADING

With winter pruning completed, the initial fertilising completed, and your main spray programme into gear, you await the first flush of spring blooms. There is always the odd bush or variety that opens before the rest, but usually most of your roses will start to bloom within two weeks of each other. This is likely to occur sooner in warm regions and later in cooler ones.

To increase the number of blooms per bush per summer, you must deadhead the bushes regularly. Once a bloom is past its best, cut back the stem that has flowered to the first strong bud – which will then produce a bloom or blooms within four to six weeks. In most regions, this means that by mid-summer a second flush of blooms will be well under way. Some people say you must cut back to the first bud where five leaflets appear. This is not always so. Certainly there is often a very strong bud at that point, but equally often you will find a bud just as suitable above.

When picking roses for a vase, always cut back to a strong bud.

HYBRID TEAS

With hybrid teas, simply deadhead to a strong bud.

FLORIBUNDAS

On the cluster-type flowerheads of a floribunda there may be a number of spent blooms, as well as blooms that have opened or are just opening and several buds that are still closed. Simply remove the spent blooms and stalks from the flowerhead.

Once the whole flowerhead has bloomed, cut back to the first strong bud. To maintain an open shape, you may sometimes need to cut back to a slightly outward-facing bud.

SUMMER PRUNING

In some districts where roses grow very strongly gardeners have rose bushes capable of reaching heights of nearly 3 metres. To control these 'giants', they reduce them by a third of their height, cutting back to a strong bud.

Some rosarians give a 'summer trim' to every stem on every bush, cutting back to a good strong bud, regardless of whether there are blooms or not. This often gives a definite autumn flush. I myself do not bother with a 'summer trim', I just keep deadheading. One reason for a 'summer trim' would be if you are going to hold a social function such as a wedding or garden party and want your roses to be at their best. If you give them a trim all over, in six to seven weeks the majority will be in bloom. How rapidly the blooms develop will depend on your autumn weather.

As autumn arrives, stop deadheading. This will encourage the rose bush to slow down, and in certain varieties to form rose hips. Glorious displays of hips are produced by some of the old-fashioned roses and many of the species varieties.

Hips are seed pods. With the correct development and processing they can therefore be used as a source from which to cultivate roses. They are known to be rich in vitamin C, and there are a number of recipes for rose-hip syrup.

The autumnal slowing down of the rose bush helps to harden the season's new growth in time for the winter. The continuation of deadheading into the autumn would encourage the plant to grow new buds, which is not desirable. Nevertheless, there are many rose varieties that, as part of their normal flowering pattern, keep blooming right up to winter pruning.

By autumn I have stopped spraying (my next spray is usually the lime sulphur after winter pruning). Autumn is the time to dig out any diseased roses, pick up the fallen rose leaves from the edges of the beds, and dig over old and new rose beds in preparation for planting new varieties in late winter.

SELECTING ROSES TO GROW

When ordering roses from growers, telephone them to confirm their closing dates for orders and place your order as early as possible. Also, check that they supply 'high-health' roses. Many woody plants, such as roses and ornamental trees and fruit trees, are propagated by budding or grafting and tend to accumulate viruses with repeated propagation. Once a plant is infected by a virus, all subsequent offspring carry it. In recent years some rose nurseries have therefore been selecting their rootstocks from sources substantially free of known viruses.

BUSH ROSES

(FL) = floribunda : (HT) = hybrid tea

'CHANELLE' (FL)

Perfect HT-shaped flowers of cream and buff, shaded with pink. Very vigorous and bushy, with healthy dark foliage and plenty of flowers.

'EROICA' (HT)

Small, dark, velvety crimson flowers with a strong fragrance. A healthy large-growing bush with lots of foliage.

'FIRST LOVE' (HT)

Very long elegant buds, opening to wide pale-pink flowers with light-apricot tonings. Marvellous for floral work, with long almost-thornless stems.

'FRAGRANT CLOUD'® (HT)

One of my favourites. The scent is superb. A free-flowering bush with a healthy medium height and bright cinnabar-red flowers.

'ICEBERG'® (FL)

One of the best of the white floribundas. It grows strongly to a large bush covered with long sprays of pure-white flowers that look lovely in flower arrangements. It has attractive light-green foliage and is extremely resistant to disease.

Left: 'Iceberg' grown as a standard.

'KERRYMAN'® (FL-HT)

Lovely HT flowers of creamy pink with deeper margins. A spreading bush with healthy foliage and a long flowering season. Because it flowers so well, it looks great planted in a mass bed and does well in a container.

'KRONENBOURG'® (HT)

Large well-formed blooms of deep velvety claret, with straw-yellow on the underside. It is a sport of 'Peace'® and has all the growth, vigour and form of its parent – but a very different colour.

Right: 'Peace'.

'MARIA CALLAS' (HT)

Another one of my favourites. I love the large full-bodied blooms of rich carmine-pink and their sweet scent. A vigorous free-flowering bush with large leathery leaves. Highly resistant to disease.

'PETER FRANKENFELDT'® (HT)

A free-flowering rose with blooms that are ideal for cutting. The long spiral buds open to large blooms of luminous cerise-pink, with a good petal texture.

'ROSENTHAL' (HT)

Another favourite, as it has tightly curled buds, a beautiful colour and an excellent scent. A dark velvety red with glowing urn-shaped buds. The flowers keep well in water when picked.

'SEXY REXY'® (FL)

An outstanding new rose that is hard to fault. The large well-spaced trusses of soft-pink blooms have an attractive form. Very free-flowering and quick-repeating, with dark-green disease-resistant foliage.

'WESTERN SUN' (HT)

A vivid deep-golden yellow, this rose has always caught my eye. The full flowers, freely borne on stiff stems, are non-fading from bud to petal drop.

It has plentiful light-green foliage and a sturdy upright habit.

Among the many other bush roses that deserve a mention are 'Burgundiaca', 'Europeana'®, 'Josephine Bruce', 'Liverpool Echo', 'Madam President', 'Margaret Merril'®, 'Pearl Drift'®, 'Precious Platinum', 'Strawberry Ice', 'Sylvia' and 'Whisky Mac'®.

CLIMBERS

CASINO'®

Large soft-yellow blooms of HT form, borne over a long period on a healthy plant of medium vigour. It has light-green foliage.

'COMPASSION'

Perfectly formed HT-type blooms of salmon-pink shaded with apricot-orange, sweetly perfumed and perfect for cutting. Very vigorous, healthy growth, with dark foliage. Repeat-flowering.

'DUBLIN BAY'®

Clusters of brilliant deep-red fragrant blooms, borne almost continuously. A strong, healthy plant with good foliage. An excellent climber.

'PARKDIREKTOR RIGGERS'®

Clusters of bright scarlet blooms, well-displayed on a large vigorous plant with abundant glossy foliage. Always in flower.

Below: 'Paul's Scarlet', a brilliantly coloured climber.

OLD-FASHIONED ROSES

'CÉCILE BRUNNER' (ROSA CHINENSIS)

Sweetheart rose, with charming small soft-pink flowers. Continuous flowering. There are both climbing and bush varieties.

'FÉLICITÉ PARMENTIER' (ALBA)

Full open soft-pink flowers that are highly scented. It has grey-green foliage. One of the best albas. About 1 metre tall.

'MADAME ISAAC PEREIRE' (BOURBON)

Large double purple-crimson flowers, borne on a big freely ranging bush. Very fragrant. I have trained one of these into a pillar rose 2.5 m high.

Below: 'Cécile Brunner'.

'SOUVENIR DE LA MALMAISON' (BOURBON)

A beautiful scented and free-flowering rose, with blush-white flowers that open to a flat quartered shape. There are both climbing and bush forms.

'SOUVENIR D'UN AMI' (TEA)

A vigorous rose that has large fragrant rose-pink double flowers. Repeat-flowering. Grows to 1.5 m.

MINIATURE WEEPING STANDARDS

These make beautiful small trees which weep right down to the ground and flower throughout the season. They look excellent in pots in courtyards and patios or in small flowerbeds.

'SNOW CARPET'®

This has miniature leaves and flowers, and a dense spreading habit. Its branches reach the ground and are covered with dainty creamy-white flowers that look like a fresh fall of snow.

'THE FAIRY'

Forms a wide-spreading and trailing head with masses of soft-pink rosette-shaped flowers in large clusters. It has beautiful shiny disease-free foliage and a good continuity of flowering.

PATIO ROSES

Over recent years a completely new type of bush rose has evolved – the patio or cushion rose. These can be very low-growing and compact or have a spreading habit. They never reach more than 60 cm, have wonderful flowers, and are extremely healthy and easy to grow. They are ideal for pots and tubs and for paved and patio areas; they can also be planted as an edging to beds and borders, and on or against low walls or along pathways.

ROSES IN CONTAINERS

For apartment blocks, town houses and small gardens, roses in tubs make an attractive display. We have five roses in clay tubs in our rear courtyard, namely 'Happy Wanderer'®, 'Hobby', 'Cécile Brunner', 'Amsterdam' and 'Wee Jock'®.

Every second or third year I remove them from their pots, give the roots a trim, and place fresh potting mix around them as I put them back into the pots. As stated above, patio roses are ideal for tubs – but you can use many of the small or medium hybrid teas and floribundas, if you wish.

TIPS FOR GROWING ROSES IN CONTAINERS:

1: Plants in pots dry out faster than in the ground, so water them more often than plants in beds.

2: Watering leaches nutrients out faster, so it is important to maintain regular feeding (one handful of rose fertiliser per month).

3: Do not use soil from the garden. It cakes hard, does not drain well, and and can prevent good root development. Buy tree-and-shrub potting mix, or mix your own.

4: Always leave a space (about 2.5 cm) below the top of the container when filling with potting mix. This allows water to pool and then soak in.

5: Make sure there are drainage holes in the base of the container. Cover these with broken pots or crockery, or large stones, then a small amount of gravel, before filling the container with shrub mix.

6: The minimum tub size needed by roses is 30 cm deep and 25 cm wide.

7: Containers are versatile; and, unless they are too large and heavy, you can move them around.

HERBS

WHAT ARE HERBS?

The word 'herb' refers to any of the host of plants, both herbaceous and woody, whose leaves, flowers, seeds, roots and bark are used for decoration, flavour, fragrance, medicine, cosmetics and dyes.

Most herbaceous plants have soft and succulent rather than woody stems. They include many vegetables, as well as flowers, shrubs, weeds and grasses. The name 'herb' derives from the Latin *herba*, meaning grass or green crops.

Below: Herbs, in this case chives, are quite happy grown among or around other plants and shrubs.

Their practicality and attractiveness make herbs a valuable asset in any garden. Tradition has dictated that herbs be planted as a separate group, either in an informal or formal herb garden or, without much imagination, alongside edibles in the vegetable garden. But times are changing!

We are now experiencing a herbal revival – a renaissance of interest in herbs due to our increased awareness of natural and healthy foods and creative cooking, as well as a resurgence of nostalgia.

Most people, after becoming aware of the pleasure and economy of home-grown produce, start out with a few basic herbs and are soon eager to try others. Nurseries are responding to this interest by offering a larger selection of new varieties, along with more of the old species.

Today, herbs are putting in appearances as part of the total garden landscape, happily planted alongside bulbs, annuals, perennials and shrubs. There are many ways that they can be incorporated into the overall garden picture: as borders or edging around beds; among annuals and perennials in flowering borders; as fillers for corners or in empty pockets between other plants; and as ground cover or as fragrant carpeting.

Herbs combine well with plants that are usually grown in rock gardens, since they thrive on hillsides and slopes or cascading over terraces. You can also use them to subdue brilliant colours, selecting species with grey or silver foliage and tucking them alongside other plants, provided that their cultivation is compatible.

Then there are container-grown herbs to move about at will, including baskets or hanging pots to suspend from roof over-hangs, tree branches, fences and walls.

Since herbs can be grown in very small spaces, you can plant creeping herbs between paving stones. Or remove a few bricks from a walkway and soften the area with creeping, fragrant herbs. Or half-bury hollow cement blocks, then fill them with plants to add interest to an open area.

There is no need think of herbs as weedy garden plants or straggly speci-mens in pots on the kitchen window sill!

Below: Herbs creeping between paving stones or spilling over concrete can look beautiful, as well as giving off a delightful scent as you walk by.

GROWING HERBS

As with most plants, the three requirements for growing herbs successfully are light, food and good drainage.

In spite of all the lore surrounding the use of herbs, growing them is no more difficult than cultivating ordinary flowers or vegetables. Most plants classed as herbs are hardy, easy to grow, practically immune to diseases and pests, adaptable to many types of soil and conditions, and quite tolerant of drought and neglect.

Like any group of plants, your attention to their simple wants and needs will be amply rewarded. Most herbs need sunlight for at least five hours a day. Some are tolerant to partial shade, and some woodland natives enjoy full shade. For the requirements of individual plants see p. 136-41.

IMPROVING DRAINAGE

In heavy soils, mix coarse grit or sand into the top 45 cm. Add compost for fibre to increase bacterial activity. This will make more plant nutrients available. It will also attract earthworm activity, which will lighten and further enrich the soil.

Most herbs, like vegetables, prefer a slightly alkaline soil. A light sprinkling of lime or wood ash will help to tone down an acidic soil. Avoid using artificial fertilisers, as these can make growth too lush. This eventually results in poor flavour and often reduces the amounts of fragrant oils stored in the leaves.

If your soil is poor, you might like to try some of the suggestions in the section on herbal fertilisers (p. 129).

Should your soil be very waterlogged or prone to becoming waterlogged, one permanent solution is to build a raised bed (widely used in traditional herb gardens).

PREPARING THE SOIL

Many herbs will survive on poor stony ground, but they generally prefer a light, slightly sandy soil with good drainage.

In a new bed, prepare the soil in early spring before sowing or planting. Dig deeply, then over several weeks remove weeds that are persistent or have taproots. Create a fine tilth, then rake it to a level surface. Let the soil settle for at least a week before planting seed. Pot-grown herbs can be planted immediately.

MULCHING

Once the herbs are established, mulching will help to prevent the soil drying out too quickly and will provide nutrients that are helpful during the growing season.

A covering of organic matter – such as bark chips, pea straw or rotted hay – spread over the soil and around the plants will control weeds and keep the soil at a cooler and more even temperature, while visually enhancing the plants' setting.

Plastic sheeting tends to make the soil's surface retain too much moisture; and since it does not allow air to circulate, the soil quickly sours.

If the soil is very moist, then herbs that prefer drier positions, such as mallows or evening primrose, may be happier with a surround of gravel rather than mulch.

Right: A healthy growth of mixed thyme.

PROPAGATION AND PLANTING

3

4

You can acquire seeds and plantlets of common herbs from garden centres, plant shops and nurseries, herb-growing friends, herb societies and mail order catalogues.

An enormous range of herbs, both common and rare, can be grown from seed; but if you require only one or two plants, it is often more economical and certainly quicker to buy them. When planting on store-bought or given plants into the garden, follow theses steps:

1 Water the soil beforehand, or let the pot soak in a bucket of water for at least half an hour to ensure that the soil and root system hold together.

2 Make a hole in the soil large enough for the plant's roots.

3 Now turn the pot upside down, with a finger on each side of the stem, touching the soil. Then give the edge of the pot a sharp rap against the edge of a bench or table. You should now be holding and supporting the plant and roots.

4 Slip the plant into the hole and check that, when the hole is filled in, the surrounding soil will come to the same level on the stem as when the plant was in the container.

5 Add a little more soil and firm it down gently to eliminate air pockets.

6 Water the firmed soil to help your new plant settle in. If you know the name of the herb, insert a label in the soil beside it.

GROWING SEEDLINGS INDOORS

For a head start on the growing season, or if you have rare or expensive seed, you may want to grow seedlings indoors. That way, all conditions can be controlled. It is not advisable to start plants with long taproots, such as parsley, indoors unless you grow them in large separate containers. Even then, they do not transplant easily.

Either use a proprietary loamless seed-growing mix or mix your own, as follows:

2 parts sterilised and sieved loam
1 part peat or leaf mould
1 part coarse sand
20 gm lime

1 Blend well and pass through an 8 mm sieve. A shallow seed tray (5 cm deep) or any clean flat container that has good drainage may be used for small seeds.

2 For small sowings, use small pots for economy of soil and space. If using deeper containers, first fill them with clean drainage material such as gravel or broken crock. Add growing mix to within 10 mm of the top.

3 Give the tray or pot a sharp downward tap. Then press the soil surface gently with a flat board. If the mix is dry, water and let it drain.

4 Sow seed thinly, mixing fine seed with some sand to help even distribution. Sprinkle a fine layer of potting mix over the seed.

5 Larger seeds should be covered with a layer of potting mix as deep as the seed width.

6 In both cases press the soil down gently, and level it if necessary. Carefully and lightly mist the soil with water, then date the planting.

7 Cover the container with a sheet of glass or plastic, or enclose it in a large plastic bag.

It should not be necessary to water again until sprouting begins, but open the cover every day for about an hour to let in fresh air and prevent moisture building up.

If dry spots appear on the soil before sprouting commences, set the containers in water until the soil is damp. This is preferable to watering them from above, which would probably flush the seedlings out of the soil.

8 When sprouting begins, take the cover off the container and place it in indirect light for several days.

9 When the first pair of true leaves has formed, after the cotyledons (the two seed leaves that emerge initially), thin out the plantlets or transplant them to a larger pot to prevent overcrowding.

10 Fill the new container with prepared seedling mix.

Handle the transplants by their leaves to prevent bruising or breaking the tiny roots and stems.

11 Using either a dibber or a pencil, make a small hole in the potting mix in the new container and set in the seedling so its leaves are 5 cm above the surface. Firm down the soil and water lightly. Set the pot in indirect sunlight.

When the seedlings have grown, remove the weaker ones and leave the strongest to continue growing. This will secure the best of the species. The herbs can now be

2

4

7

11

1

2

3

transplanted into larger pots, or planted in the garden if there is no danger of frosts.

To avoid shock to the plants, choose a calm warm day for planting out, avoiding hot, windy or rainy days. Cloches or light shelter are advisable for the early growing stages outdoors, to protect the plants from winds, unexpected frost and birds.

SOWING OUTDOORS

Annuals are best sown where you wish them to grow, as root disturbance through transplanting can make them bolt to seed.

Germination depends on three requirements: water, air and warmth. Generally, seed is sown mid to late spring, after the soil has warmed up, or in early autumn.

The appearance of new weed seedlings in the garden is a good indication that the time is right for spring sowing.

1 Remove the weeds and sow the seed thinly, either in shallow drills or freshly prepared beds. Scatter the seed evenly (if very fine, mix it with sand for better distribution) over the area.

2 Cover the seed thinly with soil, then tap it down gently. Water with a fine spray.

3 Label your beds as soon as you have planted them, so you know which plants are growing where (dill and fennel look very similar early on). Keep the soil moist, but never soggy.

Normally annuals take two weeks to germinate, and perennial herbs about three or four. Parsley is notoriously slow, taking at least six weeks until germination – so be patient.

For a continuous harvest of short-cycle herbs such as coriander and borage, make successive sowings several weeks apart. You will sometimes find that seed sown at the same time comes up in batches in various spots. This is a natural protective mechanism for survival of the species and is particularly noticeable in some wild herbs, which will grow only at certain times of the year.

PROPAGATION FROM CUTTINGS, DIVISION AND LAYERING

Cuttings are the most reliable way to get plants similar in flower colour and leaf shape to the parent plant – and the parent plant gets a beneficial trim in the process.

This method is often faster than germination from seed. It is also the most inexpensive and rewarding way to expand your herb collection. Keen herb growers are generally happy to give or exchange cuttings with other growers. Softwood, hardwood and semi-hardwood cuttings all follow the same method of propagation.

EQUIPMENT FOR TAKING CUTTINGS

You will need secateurs or a sharp knife, a clear plastic bag, damp paper towelling or something similar to keep cut ends moist (to prevent wilting), coarse sand, pumice, peat or propagation mix, and pots or deep seed trays.

SOFTWOOD OR TIP CUTTINGS

These are taken from non-woody plants. They can be taken most of the year, especially in late spring or after flowering, but not in winter. Try artemisias, balm, basil, mint, sage, thyme and hyssop.

Choose strong new shoots without any flower buds and cut straight across the shoot. The cutting should be 5-10 cm long, with four or five leaf joints. Trim the stem back to just beneath a leaf joint.

SEMI-HARDWOOD AND HARDWOOD CUTTINGS

These are taken from woody shrubs and trees. Curry plant, rosemary, rue, santolina, French tarragon and winter savory fall into this category. Cuttings from herbs such as lemon verbena can be taken from mid to late autumn.

Semi-hardwood cuttings should be 10-15 cm in length, while hardwood cuttings should be 15-40 cm long. Trim both types just below the lowest leaf bud.

Below: Rosemary in flower.

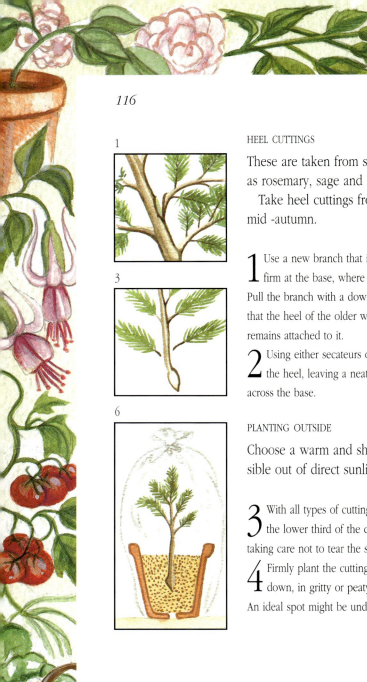

1

3

6

HEEL CUTTINGS

These are taken from shrubby herbs such as rosemary, sage and lavender.

Take heel cuttings from mid-summer to mid -autumn.

1 Use a new branch that is starting to become firm at the base, where it joins the main stem. Pull the branch with a downward movement, so that the heel of the older wood of the main stem remains attached to it.

2 Using either secateurs or a sharp knife, trim the heel, leaving a neat sliver of older wood across the base.

PLANTING OUTSIDE

Choose a warm and sheltered spot, if possible out of direct sunlight.

3 With all types of cutting, strip the leaves from the lower third of the cutting before planting, taking care not to tear the stem.

4 Firmly plant the cuttings, with the cut side down, in gritty or peaty soil and keep it moist. An ideal spot might be under the mother plant.

CONTAINER PLANTING

5 Either plant singly or place several cuttings around the edge of the pot. Insert a third of the length of each cutting into the potting medium.

6 Water and then cover with a plastic bag, raised above the leaves to prevent mildew.

This method provides the cuttings with moisture and warmth, and so helps speed up the rooting process.

7 Open the bag every few days to allow fresh air to enter and to prevent mould building up.

When the foliage seems to perk up, the bag may be removed. As soon as signs of new growth are visible (this may range from one month for tender-stemmed herbs to several months for woody-stemmed varieties), transfer the plants to containers and place them in a sheltered spot with indirect sunlight, gradually increasing exposure to direct sunlight over a period of two weeks. Apply weak liquid fertiliser or compost to provide plant nutrients.

Hardwood cuttings will develop over the winter and should be ready for spring planting. If a plant's roots show at the base of the container, either transplant it to a larger pot or plant it in its permanent position in the garden.

ROOT CUTTINGS

Root-cutting propagation of rosemary, lemon balm, sage and comfrey can be carried out in spring and autumn.

1 Dig up the plant and detach pieces of root 5 cm in diameter that have bud growth.

2 Cut these pieces into sections 5 cm long and discard the thin ends.

3 Plant them vertically in moistened potting mix in a container and cover with 5 cm of sand.

4 Cover with a plastic bag, and then follow the procedure described for container planting until there are signs of growth.

When the plants have gained substantial growth, they can be repotted or planted out in the garden.

Right: A container planted with mixed herbs.

ROOT DIVISION

This is a simple method of severing the roots so that some top growth remains attached to each piece. It is usually done with plants that grow in clumps, such as mint, bergamot, costmary, lady's bedstraw, lemon balm and yarrow.

Root division checks the spread of these herbs and keeps them hardier – as well as giving the keen gardener multiple plants for replanting or giving away. Division is best done in the spring, before there is much new growth, or in autumn after the plants have become dormant.

1 Simply wet the soil around the plant, then dig it up or take it out of its pot.

2 Separate the plant into sections either by pulling it apart with your fingers or with two forks back to back, or by cutting through sections with a spade or secateurs.

Make sure each section has a growing point and some roots. Discard hard old growth, and tidy up the plant as you go.

3 Replant the sections in the ground or in containers. Keep the soil moist until the plants have adjusted to their new situations.

Right: Planting mint in pots prevents it spreading out of control.

LAYERING

Layering involves pegging down part of a stem from the mother plant, or covering it with soil. Many plants, such as thyme often do this naturally.

Bend a stem that will touch the earth just below a leaf node that is about 10 cm from the growing tip. Peg it to the ground with bent wire or a short forked twig, so that contact is made with the soil. Keep the contact area moist, and check for root development in six weeks.

When roots are established, cut the stem from the parent just above the new roots. Dig up the newly rooted stem and plant it in a container or directly in the garden.

If you attempt layering in the autumn and your region experiences frosts, cover the contact point with mulch to prevent damage from unexpected frosts.

MOUND LAYERING

Plants that tend to become woody in the centre, such as sage and thyme, can be improved in appearance or propagated in spring by mounding soil over the woody centre until only young growth shows.

In eight weeks' time check whether new roots have developed at the base of the shoots. Once new roots are established, cut the rooted shoot from the parent plant and proceed as for layering.

Below: Sage can benefit from mound layering.

WHERE TO PLANT HERBS

Above: Nasturtiums.

HERBS FOR DRY GROUND

Dry ground, walls and earthen banks are ideal environments for most culinary and aromatic herbs, as many of them originate from harsh Mediterranean scrubland. Their volatile oils and flavours are a product of the sun and set by warm winds.

These herbs have developed colours and tough leaves to conserve moisture, which the wind and sun would otherwise evaporate. And to repel browsing animals, they have developed spiky tips, leathery surfaces and volatile oils, which form a protective vapour around the plant. In the wild these characteristics, together with their pungent flavours, help them survive the ravages of herbivores.

To simulate their natural environment, a stony well-drained garden bed, a sunny position and a not-too-rich soil are ideal.

For walls or rockeries, any herb with 'wall' in its name is an obvious choice, such as wall germander and wallflowers. Others you might like to try in crevices or on top of a sunny wall are nasturtiums, perennial chamomile, and any prostrate form of catmint, rosemary, sage or savory.

For the top of a wall, hyssop, lavender and santolina are highly suitable.

For dry corners where the soil is poor and thin, only the most tolerant and toughest of herbs – such as bugloss, mugwort, species of mallow, mullein, yarrow, evening primrose or white horehound – have the stamina to survive.

Other herbs that are suitable for dry environments include artemisias, curry plant, costmary, fennel, lady's bedstraw, hypericum, musk mallow, marjorams, weld, rue, meadow clary, salad burnet, betony, feverfew, tansy and vervain.

HERBS FOR SHADY PLACES
Generally herbs suitable for shady places are perennials that flower early and continue to have interesting foliage – a bonus when spring flowering is over and also for your overall garden plan.

FOR HEAVY SHADE: bugle, evening primrose, lungwort, pennyroyal, sweet violet, valerian and woodruff.

FOR PARTIAL SHADE: angelica, foxglove, ground ivy, lady's mantle, sweet cicely, alpine strawberries, wood sage and orris.

FOR LIGHT SHADE: chervil, chives, comfrey, foxglove, hypericum, lady's bedstraw, lemon balm, marshmallow, meadowsweet, mint, musk mallow, parsley and rocket.

HERBS FOR WATERY SURROUNDS AND DAMP GROUND
Very few herbs require a really muddy place in the garden – a reasonably water-retentive soil is usually sufficient.

The herbs mentioned below will tolerate light or dappled shade. Most of them have medicinal or household uses, and they are mostly perennials. They begin to blossom from early summer onwards.

Comfrey and elecampane will survive in a patch of damp heavy soil, if nothing else seems to grow. These are the most tolerant of herbs, growing in spreading clumps to large-sized plants. For fragrant flowers in summer, valerian, agrimony and meadowsweet do admirably. Sweet cicely, with its soft-green fern-like leaves, will put on a delicate show of white flowers in the early spring in a damp spot or beneath a tree. Other herbs for damp places are angelica, sneezewort, marshmallow and soapwort.

HERBS FOR SPECIFIC PURPOSES

SCENT

SCENTED FLOWERS

These include bergamot, calendula, chamomile, chives, evening primrose, lady's bedstraw, lavenders, lemon verbena, mallow, meadowsweet, mignonette, rocket, sages and valerian, some with delicate scents and some with powerful smells.

People often have strong personal preferences regarding scents – and what one individual finds pleasant another may find abhorrent.

Below: Chives in flower.

SCENTED FOLIAGE

Lovely when planted where they will be brushed against, these herbs release their fragrance when they are touched or picked.

They include agrimony, angelica, artemisias, anise, anise hyssop, balm of Gilead, basils, bay, bergamot, camphor, caraway, catmint, chamomile, chervil, coriander, costmary, curry plant, dill, fennel, lavenders, lemon balm, lemon grass, lemon verbena, lovage, marjorams, motherwort, oregano, pyrethrum, rosemary, rue, sages, santolina, savories, sweet cicely, tansy, thymes and tarragon, to name only some of them.

TO ATTRACT BEES

Plant the following herbs in full sun to ensure a long flowering period and a steady stream of busy workers: anise hyssop, balm of Gilead, bergamot, betony, borage, caraway, catmint, catnip, hyssop, lavenders, lemon balm, lungwort, marjoram, mignonette, rosemary, sages, savories and thymes.

TO REPEL INSECTS

The following do an admirable job in the garden and can be used to good effect indoors: artemisias, basils, chives, feverfew, garlic, mint, pyrethrum, rue, santolina and tansy.

EDGES, HEDGES, LAWNS AND GROUND COVER

FOR EDGES

Basils, chives, wall germander, dwarf lavenders, marjorams, parsleys, dwarf rosemary, rue, sages, salad burnet, savories, alpine strawberries, thyme, violets.

FOR HEDGES

Sweet bay, common sage, curry plant, hyssop, lavenders, rosemary.

FOR LAWNS

Lawn chamomile, pennyroyal and the smaller thymes.

FOR GROUND COVER

Bugle, chamomile, ground ivy, lady's bedstraw, Corsican mint, nasturtiums, oregano, pennyroyal, prostrate rosemary, prostrate winter savory, sweet woodruff and wild thymes.

FOLIAGE COLOUR

SILVER OR GREY LEAVES

Use these to lighten a dark corner, or to contrast with darker colours or to break up a colour scheme. They are very effective in mass plantings.

Herbs with silvery or greyish foliage include artemisias, camphor, catmint, clary sage, costmary, curry plant, white horehound, lavenders, mullein, pyrethrum, rue, common sage, santolina, and orange and woolly thyme.

DARK COLOURED LEAVES

Purple basil, bronze fennel, purple sage.

Below: Purple sage.

GREEN LEAVES

Anthemis (dyer's chamomile), wall germander, ground ivy, meadowsweet, rosemary and some varieties of thyme.

YELLOW OR ORANGE LEAVES

Marjoram 'Aureum', golden feverfew and some varieties of thyme.

FLOWER COLOUR

WHITE OR CREAM

Anise, applemint, basil, borage, caraway, Roman chamomile, garlic chives, Welsh comfrey, curry plant, feverfew, lemon balm, musk mallow, sweet marjoram, meadowsweet, orris, sweet cicely, winter savory, woodruff and some yarrows.

YELLOW OR ORANGE

Agrimony, calendula, chamomile, dyer's chamomile, curry plant, elecampane, evening primrose, feverfew, hypericum, lady's bedstraw, mullein, nasturtiums, santolina, tansy, woad and yarrow.

BLUE OR MAUVE

Anise hyssop, betony, borage, bugle, catmint, chives, hyssop, most lavenders, lungwort, some mints, orris, rosemary, sage, some thymes, violets.

PINK OR RED

Balm of Gilead, some basils, bergamot, betony, comfrey, coriander, lungwort, marshmallow, musk mallow, golden marjoram, motherwort, pineapple sage, red sage, summer savory, soapwort, some thymes, valerian and red yarrow.

GREEN-YELLOW

Dill, fennel, lady's bedstraw, lady's mantle, lovage, rue and weld.

HEIGHT

The height of plants helps to determine the focal point of a garden. The eye can be led to distances or corners, and takes note of features such as steps and seats, or windbreaks where provided.

The brief lists that follow give plants in order of height (with the tallest first):

EVERGREEN HERBS

Bay 7 m; box 3 m; rosemary 2.5 m; lavender 1.2 m apothecary's rose 1.2 m; Jerusalem sage 1.2 m; wormwood 1 m; southernwood 90 cm; santolina 80 cm; sage 75 cm; curry plant 60 cm.

PERENNIAL HERBS

Elecampane 2 m; lovage 2 m; sweet cicely 1.5 m; valerian 1.5 m; comfrey 1.5 m; mugwort 1.5 m; tansy 1.5 m; catnip 1.5 m; meadowsweet 1 m; fennel 1 m; marshmallow 1 m; vervain 1 m.

BIENNIAL HERBS

Angelica 2 m; mullein 2 m; weld 1.5 m; clary sage 1.2 m; evening primrose 1 m.

ANNUAL HERBS

Dill 1.5 m.

Below: A well-planted herb garden takes into account the height of the herbs when full-grown or in bloom.

CONTAINER HERBS

There are times when – because of lack of garden space or through preference or for ease of access, or to confine a plant or ensure its survival – container planting really comes into its own. It enables you to position herbs where they can delight your sense of smell, prolong their growing season, and create a visually appealing environment that is a constant source of interest. Although herbs thrive more vigorously in the ground, with a certain amount of care and common sense you can grow them in pots, either indoors or outdoors.

Below: A group of containers filled with herbs can create an attractive focal point.

When placing containers on balconies or freestanding structures, make sure that these are strong enough to support the weighty combination of soil and water. Exposure to winds also needs to be considered. Small containers may get blown over, and tender-leaved herbs can easily be damaged by strong winds.

Herbs in a group of pots can provide a focal point and look more pleasing to the eye than one lonely specimen. They also seem to enjoy each other's company and benefit from the microclimate that grouping creates. By changing the position of the pots, you can fill seasonal gaps or vary the appearance of your garden. Herbs in pots are an excellent way to create different colour schemes in small or large areas. For a silver or moonlight garden, plant artemisias, santolinas and curry plants; to create a golden garden, use lemon thyme, variegated lemon balm, calendula, lady's bedstraw, nasturtiums and variegated sage; for a blue garden, choose hyssop, borage, catmint, rosemary and sage.

The space needed by particular species will dictate how many plants can be put in a planter. A container 1 metre long can hold four or five low-growing herbs that will benefit from being kept well trimmed, such as sage, thyme, marjoram and salad burnet. A delightful addition to a barbecue area is a tub or barrel filled with culinary herbs, such as rosemary, chives, sage, mint (in its own container) or lemon balm, to add colour and fragrance to outdoor entertaining.

Remember, these plants are dependent on your care and more vulnerable than plants in the open ground. Some general rules for successful container planting are as follows:

1: Always start with a clean container. Wash it with hot water and washing soda or soap, or with a weak solution of household bleach. Then rinse well with clean water.

2: Provide the plants with good drainage. For seedlings, add some coarse pumice to the bottom of the container.

3: Make sure that the soil is friable and porous. Do not use ordinary garden soil. A good commercial potting mix is suitable for older plants, but it is often too rich for tiny seedlings. Traditional potting mixture can be made by combining 7 parts loam, 3 parts peat and 2 parts gritty or sharp sand with some well-rotted compost. Do not use builder's sand, since it will become compact and so make drainage worse. Keep the mixture loose and open to inhibit the formation of fungal spores.

4: Ensure that the sizes of the container and the plant are compatible. Small plants flounder in large pots; and, apart from looking top heavy, a pot that is too small will stifle the growth of larger herbs.

5: Check regularly for aphids and thrips, and deal with these pests if infestation is present. See the section on herbal insecticides (p. 129).

6: Check indoor herbs regularly to see if they need watering. Do not water them unnecessarily, but never allow them to become bone-dry. Rosemary never fully recovers if it dries out totally; by contrast, sage will collapse if watered too frequently.

Overwatering can cause root rot by eliminating vital air pockets needed by root hairs. An occasional spray with tepid water from a mister is useful in hot weather for soft-leaved herbs such as basil.

7: Remove deadheads, trim the leaves back, and keep the pot weed-free to aid vigorous growth.

8: Feed herbs through their leaves or the soil every two weeks during the growing season, easing off as their growth rate slows. Stop altogether during the dormant period.

9: Meet the herbs' light requirements, but do not let containers get too hot.

10: If a herb looks sorry for itself, check if it needs water or less water, or feeding, and whether it is standing in a draught or not receiving the correct amount of light.

Below: Herbs in a window box.

HERBAL FERTILISERS AND INSECTICIDES

FERTILISERS

Do not use aluminium vessels.

COMFREY

One comfrey plant will provide four crops a year. Comfrey fertiliser supplies nitrogen, phosphorus, potash and trace elements.

Method

Pick the leaves from late spring to mid-summer. Let them wilt for at least forty-eight hours, then mulch them and apply the mulch directly to plants.

Alternatively, soak fresh leaves in water for four weeks and use the liquid as a fertiliser.

DILL

This is rich in potassium, sulphur, sodium and other minerals.

TANSY

Tansy is rich in potassium and other minerals.

YARROW

Provides copper and is a good general fertiliser.

Method

Pour 1 litre of boiling water over a handful of fresh herbs or 30 gm of dried herbs, cover, infuse for ten minutes, and strain before using.

INSECTICIDES

BASIL LEAVES

These can be used to repel aphids. For method, see CHAMOMILE FLOWERS (below).

COSTMARY LEAVES

These can be used as a general insecticide. For method, see CHAMOMILE FLOWERS (below).

WORMWOOD LEAVES

These can be used against larger pests such as caterpillars, moths, flea beetles and aphids.

Because of the toxicity of wormwood, use only on mature plants.

Method

Put 15 gm of dried herbs into 1 litre of cold water. Simmer, covered, for half an hour. Then turn off the heat and steep for fifteen minutes. Do not use aluminium vessels.

CHAMOMILE FLOWERS

These prevent damping off in seedlings.

Method

Pour 1 litre of boiling water over 30 ml of dried flowers, or a handful of fresh flowers. Cover, steep for ten minutes, strain, and use at once.

PYRETHRUM

This is a natural insecticide which rapidly paralyses insects. Its flowerheads can be dried or powdered and used against all common sucking insects: bedbugs, mosquitoes, cockroaches and domestic flies. Prolonged contact with the flowerheads causes an allergic reaction in some people – so it is essential to wear rubber gloves when handling pyrethrum.

Method

Pick the open flowerheads. Dry and pulverise them. To make a spray, steep 30 gm of powder in 50 ml of methylated spirits. Dilute this with 18 litres of water.

Spray the insecticide at dusk, so plants and bees will be safe. The solution will have dispersed by morning, especially if exposed to bright sunlight.

Proprietary brands of this insecticide are also available.

Right: Basil.

PICKING AND HARVESTING

Most culinary herbs can be used from the seedling stage, as their flavours are already present. Keep in mind that, as you snip and pick, you are determining the future shape of the growing plant. If you harvest leaves judiciously, the plant will become fuller and bushier.

In general, to allow regeneration and avoid inhibiting the growth of the plant, do not remove more than a fifth of its leaves. Evergreen herbs, such as sage, thyme, basil, tarragon and marjoram, will maintain a bushier shape if the growing tip is pinched out first.

When harvesting for preserving, ensure that the herbs have not been sprayed recently with pesticides or herbicides. If they have been sprayed, always wait the time recommended by the manufacturer's instructions before harvesting.

To preserve the maximum flavour, harvest the leaves of herbs in the morning, once the dew has evaporated but before the sun has had a chance to bring out the essential oils. Gently place the leaves in a flat-bottomed basket or box, avoiding bruising them – which would lose some of the oils and so detract from the flavour.

Pick only the amount you can use in the near future. It is best to harvest only one species at a time, so that you are able to pick over the harvest for blemished leaves and then, if necessary, sort and tie the remainder into bunches.

Below: Marjoram
'Gold tip'.

Above: Harvest leaves in the morning after the dew has evaporated and before the sun has had a chance to bring out the oils.

Leaves that will be eaten as salad greens and those of borage, burnet, nasturtium, rocket, sorrel and winter savory, should be picked when young, before they flower, when they are at their most succulent.

These salad herbs, which include angelica, are not suitable for drying and can be preserved by other means. Grassy-stalked leaves such as chives and parsley should be cut or pulled just above ground level.

Aromatic evergreens such as rosemary, sage, savory and thyme all have maximum flavour just before flowering, while basil, lovage, marjoram and mint have a sweeter flavour just before they flower.

Using secateurs to harvest whole stems of small-leaved herbs speeds up collection and makes drying more convenient.

If you wish to harvest the whole plant, perennials can be cut back to half the length of the year's growth. Annuals may be cut to about 8 cm above the ground at the first harvest (in early summer), and then to ground level in autumn.

Seedheads are ready for harvesting once they have lost their green colour and feel dry to the touch, but before they have scattered their seeds on the ground. The seeds should be collected on a dry, warm day. Either shake small seeds directly into a paper bag or pop the heads or stems into bags, labelling and dating as you go. Remember to collect annual and culinary seeds for next year's propagation; and let some, such as dill and fennel, self-sow to ensure next year's crop.

Roots are best harvested in the autumn. Annual roots are harvested when their growth cycle is complete. Harvest perennial roots in their second or third year of growth, when their active components, such as volatile oils or alkaloids, have developed. After digging up the roots, take off what you require and replant the remainder to continue growing.

Most fleshy roots can be scrubbed clean, but some (such as valerian) should not be, or they will lose their active constituents.

Flowers are gathered as they fully open, the stalked varieties (such as lavenders) being snipped whole, while the others should be picked carefully to avoid wilting or damage – especially if you plan to crystallise herbs such as violets or borage.

Once picked, the flowers should be kept loose, without touching, in open containers, so as to avoid sweating and bruising. Calendula petals are removed from the flowers, while other small-headed flowers, such as chamomile, are dried intact.

Below: Basil has a sweeter flavour just before it flowers.

PRESERVING THE HARVEST

Leaves and flowers should be dried in a warm, dry, dark place with some air movement – either by hanging them upside down in bunches or by placing them on a cloth frame or wire rack.

Dry strongly flavoured herbs such as lovage separately, away from other herbs, so that their flavours do not mingle.

A loft, a sheltered garage ceiling, or an airing cupboard are all suitable places. If the drying area is dusty, or if you are drying stems with seedheads, cover the bunches with brown-paper bags loosely tied. These will act as dust covers and also catch seeds that fall off stems or out of capsules.

Drying may take as little as five days or as long as two weeks. When your harvest is ready, it will be crisp and papery to the touch. A quicker method is to spread herb leaves on a muslin-covered rack in an oven set at a low temperature, with the door open to let moisture escape.

Turn the herbs till they are crisp. Small quantities can be dried in a microwave oven, but although the flavour may not be affected, the therapeutic properties, such as those of chamomile, may be destroyed.

Roots should be cleaned, with fibrous parts removed, and cut into small even portions or segments. Dry these in a conventional oven at between 120° and 140°C, turning them at intervals until they feel fragile and can be easily broken.

Leaves should be removed from stems before being stored in labelled airtight glass or plastic containers away from light, heat, moisture and contamination. Check them periodically for damp, mould and insects, and discard them if any of these occur. When properly dried, stored herbs will retain their freshness and flavour for at least a year.

Flowers, that have been dried the same way as leaves, are best stored spread out in order to maintain their shape, especially fragile flowers such as borage and violets.

Seeds intended for culinary use should be labelled and stored the same way as leaves. Seed for sowing needs to be kept in a cool, dark place free from frost.

Roots should also be stored in airtight containers in a dark place. Those of herbs such as angelica and parsley may reabsorb air moisture – in which case, discard them if they become soft.

Other methods of preserving herbs include freezing, packing in vinegar or oil, and salt curing.

One of the most satisfying rewards for any herb grower is to be able to present a friend, neighbour or member of the family with a generous bunch of beautiful herbs, knowing that they were carefully grown, tended and harvested by your own hand.

Left: Dry your precious harvest by tying the herbs in bunches and hanging them upside down in a warm dry place.

ABBREVIATIONS: A — ANNUAL, B — BIENNIAL, P — PERENNIAL, HP — HERBACEOUS PERENNIAL, WP — WOODY PERENNIAL,
SP — SPRING, S — SUMMER, A — AUTUMN, W — WINTER, E — EARLY, L — LATE

HERB	HABIT	MAXIMUM SIZE	PROPAGATION	SPACING	COMMENTS
Agrimony, *Agrimonia eupatoria*	P. Upright, compact.	60 cm	seed – SP division – SP and A	40 cm	Self-sows readily and can become invasive. Has beautiful apricot scent.
All herb, *Coleus amboinicus*	A. Fleshy leaves, thick stems, sprawling plant.	1 m	seed – SP cuttings – SP	30 cm	Tropical plant, annual in temperate climate. Attractive as pot plant.
Alpine strawberry, *Fragaria alpina*	P. Clump-forming, compact.	30 cm	seed – SP and S division – A	20 cm	Grows well in hanging baskets, produces delicious fruit.
Angelica, *Angelica archangelica*	B. Large leaves at base, flowering stalk.	1.5 m	fresh seed – A	1 m	Large but compact, the whole plant is aromatic.
Anise, *Pimpinella anisum*	A. Slender plant.	50 cm	seed – SP	20 cm	Long warm period needed to flower.
Anise hyssop, *Agastache foeniculum*	P. Tall main stem, compact and upright.	1 m	seed – SP and A cuttings – EA	30 cm	Short-lived bee plant, with long-lasting flowers.
Mugwort, *Artemisia vulgaris*	HP. Spreading clump.	1 m²	seed – SP	50 cm	Pungent and balsamic. Self-sows readily. Can become invasive.
Common wormwood, *Artemisia absinthum*	HP. Upright-spreading fern-like plant.	1.5 m	seed – SP division – SP and A	40 cm	Will keep animals from the garden. Cut after flowering.
Roman wormwood, *Artemisia pontica*	HP. Spreading clump, dies down in winter.	40 cm²	division – SP and A	40 cm	Has deeply divided grey aromatic leaves. Keep trimmed.
Tree wormwood, *Artemisia aborescens*	WP. Compact large bush.	80 cm	cuttings – SP and A	80 cm	Good coastal hedge. Cut back in S and A.
Balm of Gilead, *Cedronella canariensis*	WP. Camphor-scented sprawling shrub.	1 m	seed – SP cuttings – SP and A	80 cm	Good bee plant. Prune regularly.
Bush basil, *Ocimum minimum*	A. Bright-green bush.	20 cm	seed – SP	20 cm	As for sweet basil. Good container plant.
Lettuce-leaf basil, *Ocimum crispum*	A. Large bright-green crinkled leaves.	50 cm	seed – SP	40 cm	Needs protection from the cold when young.

HERB	HABIT	MAXIMUM SIZE	PROPAGATION	SPACING	COMMENTS
Perennial basil, *Ocimum spp.*	P. Green compact bush.	50 cm	seed – SP	40 cm	Will not tolerate frosts or cold damp.
Purple basil, *Ocimum basilicum purpurescens*	A. Similar to sweet basil, but with purple leaves.	50 cm	Seed – SP	30 cm	Needs protection from cold when young.
Sacred basil, *Ocimum sanctum*	A. Soft hairy compact bush.	30 cm	seed – SP	30 cm	Needs protection from cold when young.
Sweet basil, *Ocimum basilicum*	A. Bright-green bush.	50 cm	seed – SP	30 cm	Protect from cold when young.
Bay (Sweet bay), *Laurus nobilis*	Compact shrub or tree.	20 m	seed – SP cuttings – SP and A	1 m	Slow-growing. Good pot plant or lawn specimen, or pruned as hedge.
Bergamot, *Monarda didyma*	HP. Spreading clump, with flowers.	60 cm	seed – SP division – SP and A	40 cm	Needs protection from frost. Cut back in A. Good bee plant.
Betony, *Stachys officinalis*	P. Compact clump, with flowers.	60 cm	seed – SP division – SP and A	40 cm	Likes semi-shade. Flowers S and A. Cut off old growth.
Borage, *Borago officinalis*	A. Very tolerant flowering plant.	1 m	seed – SP and A	1 m	Bees love its blue flowers. Self-sows freely.
Bugle, *Ajuga reptans*	P. Tolerant low-spreading plant, with flowers.	15 cm	seed – SP division – SP and A	20 cm	Good ground cover and rockery plant. Grows well in pots.
Pot marigold, *Calendula officinalis*	A. Sprawling bushy habit.	50 cm	seed – SP division – SP and A	50 cm	Cut back regularly for constant flowering. Self-sows readily. Will grow in poor soils.
Caraway, *Carum carvi*	A/B. Slender plant, grows in clump.	50 cm	seed – SP and A	40 cm	Will rot in winter if drainage is poor. The seeds are used in breadmaking.
Catmint, *Nepeta mussinii*	P. Low bushy growth, with flowers.	20 cm	seed – SP division – SP and A	50 cm	Ornamental form of catnip. Perfect foil for roses and borders.
Catnip, *Nepeta cataria*	P. Strong stems. Dies down in W.	1-2 m	seed – SP division – SP and A	30 cm	Cats drool over it. Protect young plants.
German chamomile, *Matricaria chamomila*	A. Has flowering stems.	30 cm	seed – SP and A	15 cm	Likes sun. The fried flowers make excellent tea.
Roman chamomile, *Anthemis nobilis*	P. Low spreading plant with trailing stems.	15 cm	seed – SP division – SP and A	15 cm	Beautifully scented herb for lawns, paths or banks. Prefers sandy soil.

HERB	HABIT	MAXIMUM SIZE	PROPAGATION	SPACING	COMMENTS
Chervil, *Anthriscus cerefolium*	A. Compact bright-green fern-like plant.	80 cm	seed – SP and A	20 cm	Self-sows readily. Likes cool spots. Good under deciduous trees.
Chives, *Allium schoenoprasum*	HP. Clumps of shoots from bulbs.	20-50 cm	seed – SP and S division – S and A	20 cm	Lift and divide every 2 years. Good edging and pot plant.
Garlic chives, *Allium tuberosum*	HP. Less dense clump than chives.	30-50 cm	as for chives	20 cm	As for chives.
Comfrey, *Symphytum officinalis*	P. Vigorous upright plant.	1.5 m	division – SP	70 cm	Needs to be contained. Plant out in permanent position.
Coriander, *Coriandum sativum*	A. Delicate-looking shrub-like plant.	50 cm	seed – SP and A	20 cm	Will self-sow. Unusual pungent scent.
Costmary, *Chrysanthemum balsamita*	P. Sprawling rooted clump with flowering stems.	1.5 m	division – SP and A	60 cm	Very old cultivar, also known as alecost and bible leaf.
Curry plant, *Helichrysum angustifolium*	P. Low silvery bush with flowerheads.	20 cm	stem cuttings – SP and A	30 cm	Prune lightly in ESP and A. Good edging and border plant.
Dill, *Anethum graveolens*	A. Tall feathery plant.	80 cm	seed – SP, S and A	70 cm	Needs some wind protection.
Feverfew, *Chrysanthemum parthenium*	WP. Tolerant bright-green plant.	70 cm	seed – SP and A cuttings – SP division – SP	40 cm	Self-sows readily. Cut back after flowering.
Horehound, *Marrubium vulgare*	HP. Silvery bushy growth.	50 cm	seed – LSP division – SP cuttings – S	30 cm	Some wind protection needed. Prune in SP to prevent woodiness.
Hyssop, *Hyssopus officinalis*	WP. Hardy bushy shrub.	40 cm	seed – SP cuttings – SP division – A	40 cm	Good low hedge or border plant to attract bees. Cut back in A.
Lady's bedstraw, *Galium verum*	P. Hardy delicate-looking honey-scented plant.	15 cm	seed – S division – SP and A	40 cm	Attractive and useful ground cover. A dyer's plant.
English lavender, *Lavandula angustifolia*	WP. Compact bushy grey shrub; dwarf form available.	80 cm	seed – SP cuttings – SP and A	40 cm	Beautiful hedge or specimen. Cut back after flowering.
French lavender, *Lavandula dentata*	WP. Compact bushy grey shrub with toothed leaves.	1 m	as for English Lavender	60 cm	Good medium-sized hedge plant. Flowers most of the year.

HERB	HABIT	MAXIMUM SIZE	PROPAGATION	SPACING	COMMENTS
Green lavender, *Lavandula viridis*	WP. Compact shrub, with green foliage. Distinct scent.	60 cm	as for English Lavender	40 cm	Cut back in A. Soil must be well drained.
Lemon balm, *Mellissa officinalis*	P. Tolerant bright-green shrub, grows in clump.	2 m	seed – SP and A division – SP and A	60 cm	Cut back after flowering. Self-sows easily. Can be invasive.
Lemon verbena, *Lippia citriodora*	P. Deciduous shrub.	2.5 m	seed – SP softwood cuttings – SP	1 m	Needs some shelter when young and is frost tender.
Lovage, *Levisticum officinale*	HP. Vigorous plant with tall stalks.	2 m	seed – SP and A division – SP and A	60 cm	Stately, strongly aromatic plant. Good background specimen.
Marjoram (Golden marjoram), *Origanum majorana*	WP. Low creeping golden bush. May die back in W.	10 cm	seed – SP	30 cm	Striking ground cover. Good in tubs.
Pot marjoram, *Origanum onites*	HP. Dies back in W.	50 cm	seed – SP division – LSP	40 cm	Hardy form with robust flavour.
Sweet marjoram, *Majorana hortensis*	WP. Small grey-green bush. Grow as annual.	30-50 cm	seed – SP cuttings/division – A	30 cm	Best for culinary use.
Wild marjoram, *Origanum vulgare*	HP. Forms dense mat with flowering stems.	60 cm	seed – SP	40 cm	Often called oregano. The least aromatic type of marjoram.
Applemint, *Mentha suaveolens*	HP. Vigorous spreading clump with soft green leaves.	30-50 cm	seed – SP	50 cm	Needs to be contained, looks good in large pots.
Eau-de-Cologne mint, *Mentha x piperita 'Citrata'*	P. Reddish-green flowering stems. Dies back in W.	1 m	division – SP and S	50 cm	Lovely fresh scent. Can become invasive, so needs to be contained.
Pennyroyal, *Mentha pulegium*	P. Vigorous spreading clump with flowers.	20-30 cm	seed – SP division – SP and A	30 cm	Good ground cover. Can be used for lawns.
Peppermint, *Mentha piperita*	P. Vigorous spreading clump with flowers.	60 cm	seed – SP division – SP and S	50 cm	Old culinary favourite. Needs to be contained.
Spearmint, *Mentha spicata*	HP. Creeping rootstock.	1 m	as for Peppermint	30 cm	Best culinary mint.
Curly-leaf parsley, *Petrroselinum crispum*	B. Compact clump with dark-green leaves.	60 cm	seed – SP and A	40 cm	Germination takes 4-6 weeks. Milder flavour than plain-leaf parsley.
Plain-leaf parsley, *Petrroselinum neopolitanum*	B. Compact clump with dark-green divided leaves.	70 cm	as for Curly-leaf parsley	50 cm	Very hardy strong-flavoured culinary herb. Self-sows.

HERB	HABIT	MAXIMUM SIZE	PROPAGATION	SPACING	COMMENTS
Rocket, *Eruca sativa*	A. Quick-growing salad herb.	30-70 cm	seed – SP and S	20 cm	Self-sows readily. Harvest young leaves regularly.
Rosemary, *Rosmarinus officinalis*	WP. Sprawling woody shrub.	50 cm	seed – SP cuttings – SP and A	60 cm	Good hedge plant. Keep trimmed for shape. Prefers limy soil.
Prostrate rosemary, *Rosmarinus prostrata*	WP. Trailing creeper.	15 cm	seed – SP cuttings – SP and A layering – SP, S and A	40 cm	Good hardy ground cover. Used in rockeries and hanging baskets. Slow to germinate.
Rue, *Ruta graveolens*	P. Tolerant compact pungent blue-green bush.	1 m	seed – SP cuttings – SP and S	50 cm	Prefers dry soil.
Sage, *Salvia officinalis*	WP. Short-lived bushy woody shrub.	80 cm	seed – SP cuttings – SP and A layering – SP and S	40 cm	Many cultivars, with various leaf and flower colours. Broad-leaf sage does not flower.
Clary sage, *Salvia sclarea*	B. Tall sprawling clump.	1 m	seed – SP and A	60 cm	Ornamental, needs lots of space.
Pineapple sage, *Salvia rutilans*	WP. Stems with red flowers.	1 m	cuttings – SP and A division – SP	60 cm	Frost sensitive. Cut back LW. Bees love it.
Salad burnet, *Sanguisorba minor*	P. Dainty leafy clump with flowering stalks.	20-25 cm	seed – SP and A	40 cm	Useful low border plant. Grows well in W.
Santolina (Cotton lavender), *Santolina chamaecyparissus*	WP. Compact scented bush with grey coral-like foliage.	45 cm	seed – SP cuttings – SP and A	30 cm	Good contrast and rockery plant, also makes an attractive low hedge. Trim after flowering.
Savory (Summer savory), *Satureja hortensis*	A. Compact green-red bush.	25-40 cm	seed – SP	30 cm	Sow successively for continuous harvesting.
Winter savory, *Satureja montana*	WP. Low straggly bush. Prostrate form also available.	30 cm	cuttings – SP and A layering – SP	40 cm	Cut back after flowering.
Sweet cicely, *Myrrhis odorata*	HP. Has soft green fern-like foliage.	80 cm	seed – A division – A	50 cm	Slow to germinate.
Tansy, *Tanacetum vulgare*	HP. Vigorous dark-green spreading clump.	90 cm	division – SP and A	70 cm	Very hardy. Keep under strict control. Good compost plant.
Tarragon (French tarragon), *Artemisia dracunculus*	HP. Bright-green spreading plant.	40 cm	division – SP	30 cm	Dig up and replant every 2-3 years. Needs frost protection.

HERB	HABIT	MAXIMUM SIZE	PROPAGATION	SPACING	COMMENTS
Thyme, *Thymus vulgaris*	WP. Compact dark-green aromatic bush.	30 cm	seed – SP layering – SP, S and A division – SP	30 cm	Good low hedge or border plant. Trim after flowering.
Caraway thyme, *Thymus herba barona*	WP. Green spreading ground cover.	5 cm	as for Thyme	30 cm	Good ground cover for dry areas.
Lemon thyme, *Thymus citriodorus*	P. Green spreading shrub.	20 cm	as for Thyme	30 cm	Good for rockeries and borders. Both silver and gold varieties are available.
Orange thyme, *Thymus fragrantissimum*	P. Straggly blue-grey bush.	30 cm	seed – SP cuttings – SP and A	20 cm	Keep trimmed.
Wild thyme, *Thymus serpyllum*	P. Mat-forming plant.	3-20 cm	seed – SP division – SP and A	30 cm	Excellent hardy plant for ground cover and thyme lawns.
Valerian, *Valeriana officinalis*	P. Tolerant light-green spreading clump.	1 m	seed – SP division – SP and A	30 cm	Lovely back of border plant. Flowers in second year.
Vervain, *Verbena officinalis*	P. Dark-green leafy clump. Dies back in W.	80 cm	seed – SP	30 cm	Old cultivar. Erratic germination. Cut back in W.
Weld, *Reseda luteola*	B. Low rosette in first year, flowering spikes in second year.	1 m	seed – SP	50 cm	A dyer's plant. Good for the back of borders.
Woad, *Isatis tinctoria*	B. Blue-green clump in first year, flowering stalk in second year.	1 m	seed – SP	50 cm	Unusual flat black papery rods. A dyer's plant. Good for the back of borders.
Woodruff, *Galium odoratum*	P. Bright-green aromatic spreading plant.	30 cm	seed – LS division – S	20 cm	Germination may take 12 months. Will not grow in hot dry conditions.
Yarrow, *Achillea millefolium*	P. Spreading clump, with flowers and green feathery foliage.	1 m	seed – SP division – SP and A	50 cm	Can be invasive. Good ground cover in wild areas.
Sneezewort, *Achillea ptarmica*	P. Spreading leafy clump with flowering stems.	50 cm	as for Yarrow	30 cm	Ornamental and easy to grow.

VEGETABLES

THE VEGETABLE PATCH

Growing vegetables is one of the most rewarding aspects of gardening, and is neither difficult nor as time-consuming as many people imagine.

Even in a small space it is possible to grow a wide range of nutritious vegetables – and the average back garden has the scope to produce substantial crops that will last for most of the year.

There are good reasons for adding a vegetable garden, fruit trees or herb patch to the general garden landscape. Increased knowledge about the effects of pesticides and chemical fertilisers on the food chain is a concern to many families. It is possible to supplement the average family diet with home-grown vegetables that are not only free from chemicals but rich in nutrient value due to their freshness.

A reasonable quantity of vegetables can be produced even in a small to average-size back garden. Most species can be grown much more closely together than generally indicated if the soil is rich and constantly replenished with organic matter and a good watering regime is maintained. In a larger garden partial self-sufficiency can be achieved across a wide range of vegetables if the garden is efficiently planned and maintained.

Fruit production requires more space, so it is more difficult to maintain a constant supply. But with bottling and freezing it is possible to maintain a steady supply of certain crops through the winter months.

No matter how limited, every garden should accommodate a small area to grow a few vegetables.

Below: Even a small garden usually has some space suitable for a vegetable patch.

POSITION

The most important prerequisite for growing vegetables is an abundance of sunlight. A vegetable garden needs to be located in the most open and sunny part of the garden, away from overhanging trees or shade from buildings.

This often means that the vegetable garden has to be centrally sited – a prospect that does not appeal to many gardeners. However, if the vegetable or herb patch is well cared for, there is no reason why it should not be just as attractive as an ornamental garden.

Think in terms of a kitchen garden that is located within easy access of the kitchen door. A small pathway, lined on either side with herbs, can lead to a bed containing well-mulched rows of vegetables in season.

Vine crops or root crops such as potatoes can be grown in more isolated corners (near the compost, for example), while crops that need more maintenance can be positioned in the main bed.

When choosing a site for the vegetable garden, avoid large, well-established trees.

Not only will they cast unwanted shadows; they will also compete for moisture and nutrients from the soil.

Consider the need of some crops for shelter against prevailing winds. One way of providing this is to plant a hedge of small slow-growing bushes.

Below: Consider the positioning of your vegetable patch carefully in relation to the other elements in your garden.

GARDEN PLANNING

To get the most from the available space in the vegetable garden, first draw up a garden plan. Factors to be considered when making a plan include companion planting, succession planting and crop rotation. The general rule is to alternate root crops and leaf crops, ensuring that the lower-growing species are placed at the front of the garden, where sunlight will not be blocked by larger plants.

Group perennial crops such as rhubarb, asparagus and strawberries together in one bed, where they can be mulched easily in winter time.

Allow sufficient space between rows to walk, weed and harvest. Remember, however, that if the soil is enriched with plenty of organic matter and kept well watered, then plants can be grown quite close together. Keep in mind that tall-growing crops like sweet corn, climbing beans and tomatoes should be positioned towards the back of the garden.

Use graph paper to draw a ground plan for the garden, starting with the spring growth. Record how long each group of plants takes to mature in your particular climate. After several seasons a pattern will emerge.

COMPANION PLANTING

Companion planting is a farming and gardening practice that is centuries old, but it can still be applied with great success to a modern vegetable garden.

The basic principles of companion planting are really very simple. Certain plants grow harmoniously together because their specific needs complement each other. The complex relationship between these plants can be explained scientifically, but in nature it happens spontaneously.

COMPANION PLANTING WORKS BECAUSE:

1: Shallow-rooted plants thrive when planted near deep-rooted species. The deeper-rooted plants break down and loosen the soil, providing better drainage for those with shallow roots.

2: Leaf crops do better when planted next to root crops, as they are not competing for the same ground space or specific nutrients (leaf crops need nitrogen).

3: Tall-growing species can be used to provide shade and shelter for smaller plants.

4: Species that have different water and nutrient requirements are good together, as they do not compete with each other directly.

5: Certain species have roots that give off nitrogen, making it available for nearby plants that require quantities of nitrogen to grow successfully.

6: Certain species exude aromas that repel insects, so play a useful role when planted next to plants that are susceptible to attack.

By practising the basic rules of companion planting when planning the layout of your vegetable garden, you will help to create a healthy environment – which in turn will produce plants that are less vulnerable to disease and insect pests.

Left: Companion planting will help to create a healthy environment for your vegetables to thrive.

INTERPLANTING

Make the most of the gaps in your garden, to grow some extra vegetables. The spaces between large crops, such as tomatoes, can be filled with small rows of root crops such as carrots or beetroot. Marrows or other rambling vine crops can be planted at the edge of a clump of sweet corn, and allowed to wind their way through the clump. This also works in terms of companion planting: the corn shades the marrows, and the marrow leaves stop the soil drying out around the corn.

Interplanting will only work successfully if the soil is rich and the garden is maintained to prevent weed growth. Also, in poor soil and in areas with low rainfall interplanting causes too much competition for moisture and nutrients, so none of the plants will grow successfully.

SUCCESSION PLANTING

Succession planting is the common-sense way of getting the best from your garden.

It involves planting the crops in stages, rather than all at once. Instead of planting a large quantity of each vegetable at one time, small amounts are planted every fortnight to ensure a steady supply of fresh crops.

This is especially important with leaf crops during the summer, which will all bolt and go to seed if planted at the same time. Instead of planting thirty lettuces in a single day, plant ten lettuces every fortnight, so that they will mature and be ready for harvesting over a much longer period. Without succession planting, all thirty will need harvesting at the same time, creating a glut.

Succession planting saves ground space, because as each row is harvested a new crop can replace it.

In a cool or cold climate, succession planting is limited to some extent by the length of the spring and summer growing season – especially since crops such as tomatoes or capsicum need to be planted in early spring if they are to have time to mature before the autumn.

In warmer climates, with a less dramatic difference between seasons, succession planting can be practised all year round, providing a steady supply of fresh crops.

CROP ROTATION

This is yet another horticultural practice that has been used for centuries. Long before any scientific explanations were available, farmers knew from experience that planting crops in the same field year after year yielded poor results. Soil-borne diseases could be transferred from one season's crop to the next, so a rest or fallow period became necessary.

Although not used as often as it should be in agriculture, crop rotation is certainly advisable in the vegetable garden. Certain crops demand specific nutrients from the soil, and if these crops are grown in the same spot season after season the soil balance will be depleted.

Leaf crops draw nitrogen from the soil in large quantities. Therefore a leaf crop should always be followed by a root crop that does not demand as much nitrogen.

In your garden always plan to change the layout every year (A), so plants from one family group are not always positioned in the same place. For example, cabbage, Brussels sprouts and cauliflower all belong to the same family group and should therefore be moved every year. Using this system, nutrient deficiencies can be prevented, since different plant groups take different nutrients from the soil. By rotating root and leaf crops, a balance is achieved. Also, pH requirements vary from plant to plant.

Do not position acid-loving plants in ground that has been limed. Follow a heavy-feeding crop with one that requires less nutrients from the soil.

To create a productive vegetable garden, the starting point is ensure that you have rich friable soil. Vegetables are generally heavy feeders and therefore require good soil. Plants grown in poor soil are much more susceptible to insect attack and to disease infestation. They also tend to grow slowly and become woody and tough.

A

year 1   year 2   year 3

PARSLEY

DILL

SAVORY

CHIVES

BROCCOLI FOLLOWED BY CORN,
PLANTED WITH LETTUCE AND RADISHES

PEAS FOLLOWED
BY BEANS

SPINACH FOLLOWED
BY BEANS FOLLOWED
BY CAULIFLOWER

PEAS FOLLOWED BY
CUCUMBERS PLANTED
WITH RADISHES

EARLY LETTUCE
FOLLOWED
BY MELONS

CARROTS PLANTED
IN SUCCESSION

TOMATOES PLANTED
WITH COS LETTUCE,
RADISHES OR SHALLOTS

CABBAGE FOLLOWED
BY SQUASH

MUSTARD GREENS
FOLLOWED BY PEPPERS
PLANTED WITH LETTUCE

BEETS FOLLOWED
BY BROAD BEANS

BROCCOLI FOLLOWED
BY BEANS FOLLOWED
BY TURNIPS

PARSLEY

CHIVES

DILL

BASIL

MARJORAM

TARRAGON

A workable example of crop rotation and interplanting of leaf, vine and root crops

SOIL IMPROVEMENT

TYPES OF SOIL

In order to improve the soil, first assess its texture and drainage qualities. Soils fall into the following categories:

SANDY SOIL

This is light and easy to cultivate, but loses moisture too quickly, becoming dry and often hard-caked on the surface. It is difficult to form into a shape. It will crack and crumble, and if you try to bend the shape it will fall apart.

Add plenty of well-rotted manure, compost or other soil-building materials, such as rotted leaves.

LOAM

This is the ideal soil to find in your garden, as it is easy to cultivate yet holds moisture well.

Good loam has neither too much sand nor too much clay content. It forms a shape much more easily than sandy soil, and holds together quite well. However when you try and bend the shape, it will crack slightly.

CLAY

This type of soil is heavy and hard to work. With a clay soil, water takes a long time to drain away after rain or watering.

To test the texture of your soil take a small quantity – half a handful – and lightly moisten it. The object of this test is to form the soil into a sausage shape, then lightly bend it, to determine its structure.

To improve the structure and texture of the soil, the addition of plenty of organic matter is essential. There are clay-breaking substances, such as gypsum, which are useful to help break down clay particles.

DRAINAGE PROBLEMS

Drainage can affect the health of vegetables that rot in poorly drained conditions. Areas of the garden with poor drainage need to be corrected.

Badly drained soil is generally easy to identify, as the structure tends to be heavy and the soil is frequently very wet.

However, if you are uncertain about drainage, try this simple test. Dig a hole to a depth of about 60 cm and fill it with water until the entire area appears to be saturated. If your drainage is adequate, the water in the hole should drain away in a few hours. If it remains in the hole till the next day, poor drainage is the reason.

Layered compost that includes manure will break down quickly

SOIL
MANURE
SAWDUST
WASTE VEGETATION
SOIL
MANURE
SAWDUST
WASTE VEGETATION
SOIL
MANURE
SAWDUST
COARSE VENTILATION

Right: Compost added to the soil will help ensure that the plants gain the nutrients they need.

Poor drainage can be solved in various ways. The simplest is to improve the texture of the soil by adding organic matter such as manures and compost; or you can create built-up beds that incorporate their own drainage. Because good drainage is so vital, vegetable gardeners frequently use built-up beds.

An alternative solution is to lay underground drainage pipes to direct water away from the plant roots. This is not as difficult as it sounds, although digging trenches may involve some back-breaking labour. The pipes need to be laid at a slight angle, sloping downwards. When too much water hits the subsoil, it drains through a bed of gravel into the pipes, which carry it away to lower ground.

Organic gardeners sometimes plant deep-rooted species such as comfrey or lupins in the badly drained area. When mature, the plants can be chopped with a spade and dug into the ground together with lots of well-rotted manure. In the meantime, while the plants are maturing, their roots help to break up the subsoil.

SOIL BUILDING

It may take several years to build healthy soil by incorporating organic matter. But, regardless of the original soil condition, the addition of composts and manures will result in a marked improvement and generally makes gardening much easier.

Apart from adding valuable nutrients to the soil, incorporating organic matter improves texture, structure and drainage, and makes cultivation easier.

It is always best to incorporate composts and manures into the soil before planting. After planting, an additional application as a thick mulch layer will gradually break down into the soil and, as it decomposes, will release valuable nutrients as well as improving texture and drainage.

Vegetable gardens are often considered time-consuming because most species of vegetables are annuals. It is argued that they must therefore be labour intensive, demanding frequent planting, mulching, weeding, watering, feeding and harvesting.

In fact, a well-planned vegetable garden should require no more than a routine weekly maintenance taking about two hours for most of the year. It is true that there are times when the work may be greater – particularly in early spring, when time is needed to clear away winter debris and plant summer crops. But on a regular basis a few hours work should be enough to keep the garden in good order.

PLANTING

To maintain a steady supply of vegetables, routine planting of either seeds or seedlings is required.

Plant according to the seasons – and only plant a consumable quantity of each variety at a time, to avoid a glut (see SUCCESSION PLANTING, p. 148).

WEEDING

Routinely keep weeds down between rows, using a hoe or cultivator. To make weeding easier, water the ground well the day before. Take care not to disturb the root systems of young plants.

MULCHING

This is excellent to reduce weed growth and to prevent the soil surface drying out. Mulch between rows and around plants, applying a thick layer of well-rotted manure (poultry, cow or horse); and then on top of it spread a layer of grass clippings. Maintain the mulch layer every few weeks.

A well-mulched vegetable patch.

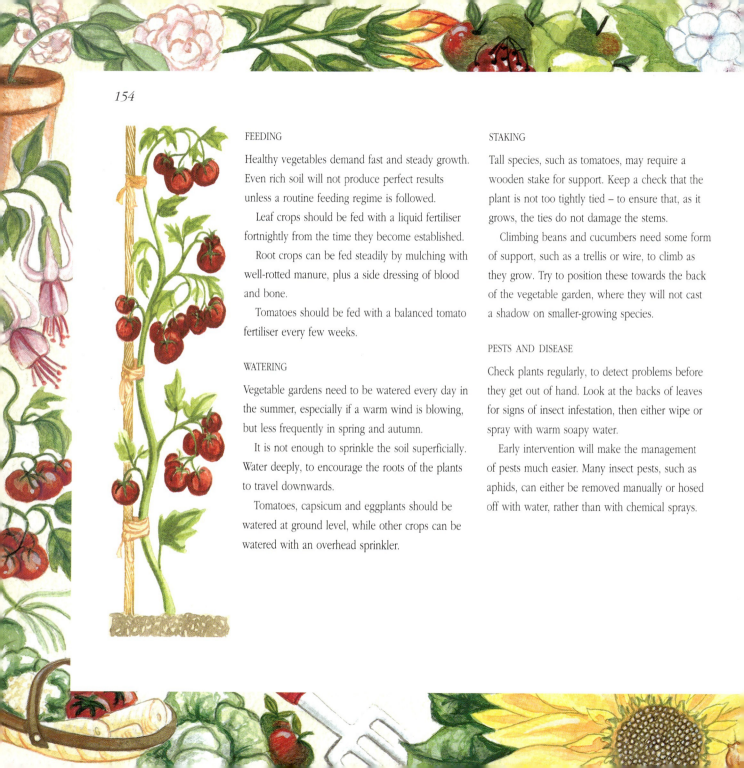

FEEDING

Healthy vegetables demand fast and steady growth. Even rich soil will not produce perfect results unless a routine feeding regime is followed.

Leaf crops should be fed with a liquid fertiliser fortnightly from the time they become established.

Root crops can be fed steadily by mulching with well-rotted manure, plus a side dressing of blood and bone.

Tomatoes should be fed with a balanced tomato fertiliser every few weeks.

WATERING

Vegetable gardens need to be watered every day in the summer, especially if a warm wind is blowing, but less frequently in spring and autumn.

It is not enough to sprinkle the soil superficially. Water deeply, to encourage the roots of the plants to travel downwards.

Tomatoes, capsicum and eggplants should be watered at ground level, while other crops can be watered with an overhead sprinkler.

STAKING

Tall species, such as tomatoes, may require a wooden stake for support. Keep a check that the plant is not too tightly tied – to ensure that, as it grows, the ties do not damage the stems.

Climbing beans and cucumbers need some form of support, such as a trellis or wire, to climb as they grow. Try to position these towards the back of the vegetable garden, where they will not cast a shadow on smaller-growing species.

PESTS AND DISEASE

Check plants regularly, to detect problems before they get out of hand. Look at the backs of leaves for signs of insect infestation, then either wipe or spray with warm soapy water.

Early intervention will make the management of pests much easier. Many insect pests, such as aphids, can either be removed manually or hosed off with water, rather than with chemical sprays.

THE CROPS

LEAF CROPS

To be light and crisp leaf crops should be grown quickly, with plenty of watering and feeding to maintain steady growth.

CELERY (*APIUM GRAVEOLENS*)

This crop requires plenty of water and regular feeding to provide the rapid growth necessary for success. Stalks should be blanched to remain light green, and this involves either wrapping the base of each plant in newspaper or planting seedlings in a trench, then gradually filling around the base with soil as the plant grows.

CRESS (*LEPIDIUM SATIVUM*)

Cress is best produced under glass for rapid tender shoots, either in a fine soil or on an absorbent pad (the latter eliminates gritty soil particles). Feed fortnightly, and harvest by clipping back with sharp scissors. It only takes a few weeks to begin producing sufficient for a daily salad!

DANDELION (*TARAXACUM OFFICINALE*)

Although considered a weed, dandelions are very nutritious and can be used in salads. Collect seeds and sow a small patch in the vegetable garden. They require no special care or attention.

ENDIVE (*CICHORIUM ENDIVIA*)

A late-autumn alternative to lettuce, endive has a high iron content and a slightly bitter flavour. It needs protection against frost and, like celery (see left), should be blanched before harvesting.

LETTUCE (*LACTUCA SATIVA*)

Choose from many varieties of cos and cabbage lettuce. Lettuce can be grown most of the year, using greenhouses in cool regions. Begin outdoor sowing in spring once frost danger has passed.

Below: Leaf crops such as lettuce should be watered regularly and grown quickly to ensure their crispness.

SILVER BEET (*BETA VULGARIS CICLA*)

Easy to grow, this is an excellent crop for small gardens because it produces a vitamin-rich yield in a small space. Leaves can be harvested individually by cutting with a sharp knife right at the base. In warm regions, plant seeds every month for a year round supply.

SPINACH (*SPINACIA OLERACEA*)

Prefers a cool to cold climate and rich moist soil. Plant as a catch-crop between rows of beans, cabbages or leeks. Outer leaves should be ready for picking after only eight weeks.

Below: Cabbage.

THE BRASSICAS

Most brassicas are heavy feeders. They need to be grown quickly to produce tender results, as slow growth will result in woody crops. Brassicas are prone to insect attack by cabbage moth, caterpillars and other leaf-eating pests, but a few preventative measures (derris dust is a good all-round deterrent) should enable them to withstand the onslaught, if well grown.

BRUSSELS SPROUTS (*BRASSICA OLERACEA 'GEMMIFERA'*)

These take up quite a lot of space in the garden, but are a good crop for the autumn and winter months. Sprouts grow best in cool to cold areas, where seeds can be sown from late spring to late summer. In warm to tropical districts sowing should be left until late summer.

CABBAGE (*BRASSICA OLERACEA 'CAPITATA'*)

There are many varieties to choose from, including some that crop after only seven or eight weeks.

The leaves have a high water content, so regular watering and feeding is necessary. Cabbages can be grown all year round with succession planting (see p. 148), but do not stand severe frost.

CAULIFLOWER (BRASSICA OLERACEA 'BOTRYTIS')

Cauliflowers are very heavy feeders, so add plenty of manure to the soil before planting and mulch well. Seeds can be sown in late summer in most regions (in warmer climates extra watering will be needed).

When the heads begin to form, tie the outer leaves together to cover them, as this will keep the heads snowy white. Broccoli is a close relative.

KOHL-RABI (BRASSICA OLERACEA GONGYLOÏDES)

Tasting a bit like a cross between a swede and a turnip, kohl-rabi forms a bulb above the ground, topped with cream-and-purple foliage. The small form is suited as a catch-crop, the larger is coarse and grown for cattle fodder.

Relatively easy to grow, both bulb and foliage are edible, and should be ready to pick in about eight weeks after sowing.

SWEDES (BRASSICA RUTABAGA)

Swedes are a winter crop that requires rich moist soil. Seeds can be sown from mid-summer in cold areas, or late summer in warm regions.

Although quite slow-growing, swedes store well in a clamp, and the crop can be made to last for many months.

TURNIPS (BRASSICA RAPA)

Turnips are a winter crop, and seeds should be sown in spring for an early crop or mid-summer for a late crop.

A mulch of well-rotted manure topped by grass clippings will keep down weeds. Rich moist soil produces good results.

ROOT CROPS

Generally not as demanding on the soil as other crops, root crops need good drainage.

BEETROOT (BETA VULGARIS)

Beetroot is best when picked and eaten young. It likes a rich soil, high in nitrogen. Poultry manure dug in prior to planting is therefore beneficial. Also, add a sprinkling of lime and mulch well once the seedlings have reached 10 cm in height. Force growth along with regular feeding and watering, and begin pulling every second plant eight to ten weeks from sowing.

CARROTS (DAUCUS CAROTA)

The average harvesting time for carrots is at least sixteen weeks, and seeds can be sown from early spring in most areas. Successive outdoor sowing will extend your harvest.

Because carrot seeds are very small, the main problem is sowing them thinly enough. Try mixing some seeds in a salt shaker with some dry sand. Sprinkle this mix along a row and cover with light soil, then keep moist until germination.

Even with this method, the seedlings will need to be thinned to prevent overcrowding.

Well-developed roots can be stored in a clamp or sand box for winter use.

PARSNIPS (*PASTINACA SATIVA*)

The distinctive taste of parsnips tends to be either loved or hated. Follow the same planting procedure as for carrots. They need to be grown quickly and harvested when young, or they will develop a tough, stringy texture.

Below: Root crops invariably need good drainage.

Lift when the leaves die down and store in a clamp. Lifting after a frost is thought to improve the flavour.

POTATOES (*SOLANUM TUBEROSUM*)

Because of limited space, potatoes tend not to be grown in suburban vegetable gardens. However, home-grown potatoes are so good that it is worthwhile devoting a section of the garden to them.

Nurseries sell seed potatoes in many varieties. Or try planting left-over kitchen potatoes that have begun to sprout.

Surprisingly, potatoes like rich well-drained but moist soil. They can be grown all year round in temperate to hot zones. In cooler regions sowing can begin in spring, after the frosts have finished.

When the foliage appears, mulch well; then continue mulching to prevent the potatoes emerging from beneath the ground (once exposed to light they turn green and cannot be eaten). Ensure they are lifted and stored before risk of frost.

SWEET POTATOES (*IPOMOEA BATATAS*)

Sweet potatoes take a long time to grow and must have a long, hot summer. In cool regions it is hard to get good results, because the growing season is too short. They are very rich in vitamins.

Seed stock is hard to find, but it is possible to grow tubers from bought produce that has been allowed to shoot. An average sweet-potato plant takes five months to mature.

VINE CROPS

These are best sown directly where the plants are to grow. The most effective method is to create a small hill with a dish-shaped centre.

Sow at least three seeds in this 'dish' and keep lightly moist until germination. After a week select the strongest plant, then remove the remaining ones.

Mulch well, taking care not to take the mulch too close to the stem – which can create too much humidity and cause a fungal disease.

CUCUMBER (*CUCUMIS SATIVUS*)

In warm regions cucumbers can be grown from seed sown directly in the ground. In cool regions they are best reared under glass.

Add well-rotted manure and lime or dolomite before planting. Avoid overwatering during the germination period, but water well once the plants are established. Shade from direct sunlight.

PUMPKINS (*CUCURBITA MAXIMA*)

To do well pumpkins need a rich moist soil, protection from frost, and a long hot summer. Sow seeds in early spring, and in cool regions bring the plants on under glass. Water and feed regularly throughout the growing season.

Mulch around the seedlings once established, as competing weeds will slow down growth.

Although the smaller varieties may be ready for harvesting after four months, the larger types take longer. Wait until the foliage and stems have withered before harvesting.

SQUASHES, MARROWS AND COURGETTES (*CUCURBITA PEPO OVIFERA*)

These fast-growing summer crops are grown easily from seed sown in early spring. Sheltered sunny sites give the best results.

Once established and mulched, they need very little attention apart from watering. The flowers are also edible, but it's worth waiting for the squashes.

Once the squashes start to form, growth is rapid – so check progress daily, as regular harvesting encourages new growth.

THE ONION FAMILY

The vegetables in this group are easy to grow. They have no particular growing requirements and produce a good quantity in a small space. There are now varieties suitable for all climates.

CHIVES *(ALLIUM SCHOENOPRASUM)*

Chives grow quickly in moderately rich moist well-drained soil. The grassy foliage produces pretty purple flower-heads, which will self-seed for the following season. Cut chives at ground level as needed, using sharp scissors.

LEEKS *(ALLIUM PORRUM)*

Leeks need richer soil than other members of the allium family. They prefer a cool to cold climate, although they will grow in warmer areas if seeds are sown in autumn. Consider using plots vacated by early harvests of pea, potato and salad crops.

Make a trench and sow the seeds at the bottom. The stems need blanching as the plants grow; this involves covering the base of the stems with soil to keep them white. Mulch well and water regularly.

SHALLOTS *(ALLIUM ASCALONICUM)*

Shallots prefer cool growing conditions. In warm regions they should be planted in autumn; in cool regions, plant in spring. The soil should be moderately rich and well drained. Once established the seedlings need to be thinned and mulched.

Harvest as the foliage turns yellow. Lift and lay in the sun for two or three days, then store in a cool dry place or pickle in vinegar.

PEAS AND BEANS

Both peas and beans have the same basic growing requirements. The soil for both needs to be rich with organic matter and well drained, with some lime or dolomite added prior to planting seeds.

FRENCH BEANS *(PHASEOLUS VULGARIS)*

Since they are climbers, French beans are a good space-saving crop for small gardens. They need moderately rich soil. Add lime before planting.

Once seeds are established, mulch and water well; then feed fortnightly once the flowers appear.

Harvest when the beans are young and tender; they will quickly become tough if left on the vine.

In warm climates, successive sowing will keep a good supply going.

BROAD BEANS (*VICIA FABA*)

This is a cool-climate crop that can be sown in spring for summer harvest and allowed to mature as the weather cools in autumn.

Beans are heavy feeders and need plenty of ground space. Mulch the seedlings well and water frequently during warm weather.

Once the pods begin to form, pinch back the tips of the foliage to encourage faster maturing.

PEAS (*PISUM SATIVUM*)

Peas are a good cool-season crop. Soil should be rich and sprinkled with dolomite before planting. Sow the main crop in spring. Staking will allow light and air to circulate around plants. Keep well watered during dry spells.

Depending on the variety, peas mature in twelve to sixteen weeks. Crops are reduced if left on the vine. Peas are best picked and eaten when young.

SUMMER CROPS

Salad crops such as sweet peppers (capsicum), eggplants (aubergines), sweet corn and tomatoes are best grown in summer, even in warm regions. All require plenty of space, good rich soil and lots of sun to produce good results.

SWEET PEPPERS (*CAPSICUM ANNUM*)

Plant early in spring, as capsicums need a long hot summer to ripen.

In cool regions wait for frosts to pass, then plant in a sheltered sunny site. Stake as the fruits form.

Mulch, water and feed plants well. Pick late in the summer season.

Below: Beans grown over a frame.

EGGPLANT (*SOLANUM ORIGERUM*)

Grow eggplants (aubergines) under glass in cool regions. Rich well-drained soil is needed. Mulch and water plants well in summer.

As the fruits begin to set, start a weekly feeding regime. Maintain four to six fruits on each plant, to encourage a larger and healthier crop. Harvesting can begin after fourteen to sixteen weeks.

Below: Sweet corn.

SWEET CORN (*ZEA MAYS*)

Corn needs plenty of space and good rich soil to be effective. The seeds should be sown directly into the ground, in a block of short rows for easy germination. In cool regions sow groups of three seeds under glass in spring, then prick out the two weakest plants later.

When the seedlings emerge, mulch well. A layer of grass clippings will help to keep down weeds.

Water and feed regularly. Start checking husks when the silks turn brown – do not leave ripe corn on the stalks or it will become woody.

TOMATOES (*LYCOPERSICON ESCULENTUM*)

Tomatoes need as much sun and air as possible. In cold climates, bring on seedlings under glass. For a summer crop, plant out in late spring in a warm, sunny sheltered position.

Mulch around the young seedlings, and water regularly at ground level (the plants can develop disease if their foliage is constantly wet).

A larger crop is assured if the lateral growths are pinched back from an early stage, encouraging only fruiting stems to develop. In warm climates well-grown tomatoes should be ready for picking after twelve weeks.

PERENNIALS

Perennial crops should be grown in an area of their own, where they can be covered with a good mulch of well-rotted manure during the winter while growth is dormant. The most popular perennials are rhubarb, artichokes and asparagus, which emerge from the ground in early spring then die back completely in winter.

ARTICHOKES (*CYNARA SCOLYMUS*)

Freshly picked artichokes are delicious, and just a few plants in the garden are well worth the space.

They are best grown in temperate zones, as they resent conditions that are either too hot or too cold. Fast growth is essential, so make sure the soil is rich and moist; it also needs to be well-drained.

Plant out on a sunny but sheltered site. Water and feed regularly during the main growing season (spring and summer).

ASPARAGUS (*ASPARAGUS OFFICINALIS*)

Asparagus require a hot summer and cold winter, although they can be grown quite successfully in most areas.

Make sure the soil is rich before planting the crowns, and mulch well in winter. Since they are quite heavy feeders, regular applications of liquid plant food will be beneficial.

The spears emerge in spring. Regular harvesting will extend the season.

RHUBARB (*RHEUM RHAPONTICUM*)

If well tended, rhubarb produces vigorous stalks over many months.

Give rhubarb a surface mulch in winter, while the crowns are dormant, using well-rotted manure to enrich the soil.

In the spring begin a regular watering regime, as the stalks have a high water content; continue mulching and watering through summer. Harvest the outside stems from late spring onwards.

Left: Rhubarb needs to be watered regularly in the spring.

PRUNING

BASIC TECHNIQUES

To be a successful gardener, it is essential to understand how plants grow and when and how they need to be pruned.

Not all plants require regular pruning. It depends on the way they grow. However, all plants, shrubs and trees do need to be groomed to remove dead or broken parts.

GROWTH PATTERNS

All flowering plants are built to the same basic plan. Shoots that consist of a series of joints (nodes) are separated by unjointed internodes. Initially nodes usually bear a leaf or leaves. Buds (which are embryo shoots) occur at the shoot tip and in each leaf axil.

Once leaves have fallen they are not replaced and the stems may become bare, but in many plants the buds left behind grow into new leafy shoots. However, the stems of some evergreens (for example, most of the conifers and Proteaceae) have live auxiliary buds only where there are still leaves, and cutting back to leafless wood causes the death of the cut shoot.

In some shrubs a single trunk rises from the roots, while others have a suckering habit and produce a thicket of stems. As new growth develops old stems die, so clumps become choked with dead growth.

Flowers usually develop on young growth. Shoots of non-woody perennials commonly die after producing seeds, to be replaced by others that develop from buds at the base.

In many woody plants flowers grow on side shoots, whose buds then shoot and flower in turn. As a result, growth tends to become crowded and feeble.

In a few families, as well as the buds that develop in the leaf axils, each year at the end of the growing season a ring of buds forms just below the tip of each shoot. When growth begins again, side shoots form from these buds only, so that the branches are arranged in whorls. Eventually these side shoots in turn develop whorls of branches. On plants with whorled growth, the leaf-axil buds do not normally give rise to shoots, but they may be induced to grow if the stem is damaged or pruned.

In families with whorled branches, the growth after flowering follows one of two distinct patterns. One type can be seen in members of the Myrtaceae family that have bottlebrush-like inflorescences, such as callistemon and beaufortia, which produce their flowers not on side shoots but directly on the main stem. Each stem continues to grow beyond the flowers and may produce its next whorl of branches just above the inflorescence. The site of the old inflorescence may be marked by a bare section of stem, but in some species woody seedcases remain clinging to the stem.

Another type of growth is common to rhododendrons and proteas in particular. At the end of the growing season of these plants a flower bud forms at the tip of the shoot, with a ring of growth buds below it. The shoots that have formed inflorescences do not grow any further, but once flowering is over the vegetative buds beneath the flowerhead develop into a whorl of new branches. As this pattern is repeated at every flowering, the stems become widely spread out. Some varieties do not flower for several years after planting. If no flower bud occurs at the shoot tip, a vegetative bud develops instead. In spring this bud grows into an extension of the main shoot, but side shoot development does not occur. Plants that do not flower therefore tend to develop long, lanky, bare stems. However, in almost all rhododendrons and some proteas live buds remain even on old wood. Cutting back will activate them, so severe pruning is a recognised method of rejuvenating old, straggly bushes.

Below: Correct pruning procedures help to ensure a colourful display.

REDUCING HEIGHT

A. Alternate branching

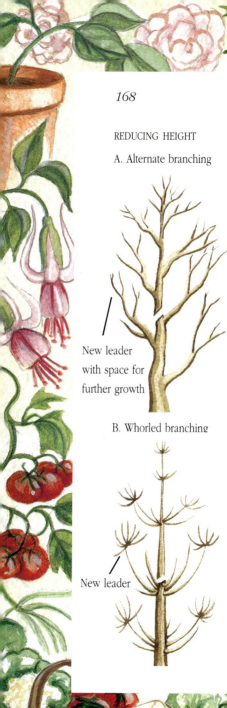

New leader with space for further growth

B. Whorled branching

New leader

A few shrubs and trees flower on spurs. These are specialised, much-compressed side shoots, sometimes branched, which live for many years, growing very little but bearing flowers annually. Since the spurs take time to establish, the tip wood rarely bears flowers.

Most shrubs and trees have one annual growth period – which is straight after flowering – and then form new terminal buds. The new wood hardens progressively, until by the winter it is firm enough to snap and has a distinct bark.

The new wood is usually distinguished from older wood by a different colour, smoothness and lack of branching. Sometimes the junction between the new and old wood is marked by ring-shaped scars. In plants that have main shoots only, each whorl of branches is a record representing one season's growth.

PRUNING TERMS

HARD PRUNING

Removing half or more of the season's growth.

LIGHT PRUNING

Removing one-third or less of the season's growth.

PINCHING OR STOPPING

Nipping the soft tips with the fingers.

STUBBING OR STUBBING BACK

Cutting a shoot to within two or three buds of its base.

WATER SHOOT

A strong sucker on the main framework of a single-stem woody plant.

PURPOSEFUL PRUNING

Many young plants are pruned to stimulate branching, as well as to achieve more compact growth. Not all branch freely, so long bare stems may develop.

Auxiliary buds may fail to shoot because they are suppressed by hormones from the terminal bud. When the terminal bud is pruned off, this effect vanishes and several shoots may develop. Usually the top bud becomes dominant and forms a new leader. Buds further down are usually influenced by the new tip to grow out sideways, but the one immediately below the top shoot may challenge it for dominance, forming an undesirable double head. Remove this second shoot, or else prevent the problem ever occurring by destroying its bud at the first pruning. In many trees buds grow in a spiral around the stem (A and B), and shoot development can be directed according to which buds are stimulated to grow.

The influence of a terminal bud on any shoot in the formation of laterals is diminished if the shoot is bent until it is nearly horizontal. This is why horizontal training is an effective way of encouraging the development of flowers along the stems of climbing roses and other climbing plants.

The result of pruning a shoot depends on how it is cut. If it is made on a length of stem with dormant buds it is likely that several will form shoots. Usually the more severe the cut, the more vigorous the subsequent growth. This technique is used to thicken hedges. Cuts should be made just far enough from nodes to avoid damaging them. Since lengths of internode have no leaves to draw sap they soon die, leaving an unsightly snag that sometimes leads to extensive dieback.

Pruning may curtail growth (C). Where the node nearest the cut already bears a side shoot, buds further back are not usually activated and the shoot takes over as the head of the stem or branch. This allows leading shoots and laterals to be shortened without obvious mutilation or stimulating unwanted shoots.

Having to prune a tree or shrub down to size is usually a sign of poor planning, although some are trained deliberately for special effects or tailored to fit awkward spaces. All plants grow both sideways and upwards, which needs to be allowed for when planting. The worst problems often seem to occur beside paths and walkways or below overhead wires!

MAJOR SURGERY

Sometimes it is necessary to amputate large tree limbs (D). This should never be attempted by amateurs unless the limb can be reached comfortably from the ground, or without difficulty from a secure ladder. For safety, branches that are so high that

C. Curtailing spread

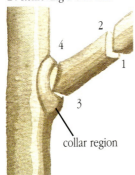

D. Removing a tree limb

collar region

(cuts numbered in order)

they can only be reached by climbing or with special equipment should always be dealt with by a qualified arboriculturist, who can advise on health problems that often make old trees unsafe.

It is essential to make the cut correctly if proper healing is to take place. Snags and torn bark both lead to rot and, apart from being unsightly, can eventually make trees dangerous. At the base of every branch is a slightly swollen region known as the collar. It has been found that if this is left intact, the tree is able to resist rotting and usually the bark eventually heals, so that the wound is no longer visible. A collar occurs even on small branches, so when removing any branch care should always be taken to retain it.

If bark is to heal over successfully, it must form a smooth ring around the wound. This can be achieved with two saw cuts: the first, quite shallow, beneath the branch, and a second from above down to meet it. This will prevent a tear at the base of the wound, which is unavoidable when branches of any size are removed with a single cut. A big limb should be reduced to a half-metre stub before the final operation – and for extra support, tie it to the branch above.

Smooth the cut bark with a sharp knife to promote healing. Wound protection is now no longer recommended except when pruning species (such as prunus species and silver birches) that are susceptible to silverleaf fungus – in which case, a fungicidal pruning paste should be used.

TOOLS

Only prune with the correct tools, and make sure they are properly maintained. Not only is it inconvenient to struggle with substandard equipment, but tearing and bruising prevent plant tissues healing and so make plants vulnerable to disease.

Secateurs should only be used for small stems, no more than 15 mm in diameter. Most secateurs work well, but the lighter types are intended for cutting flower stems rather than for pruning.

Stems with a diameter of 15 to 25 mm can be cut with long-handled loppers. Handle strength is important: light aluminium loppers tend to bend out of shape.

Always keep these tools clean and sharp. Blades will be coated with plant juices, so after use they should be rubbed with fine steel wool, then lightly oiled.

Larger garden centres sometimes offer a sharpening service, but it is not difficult to sharpen tools at home, using an oilstone or a butcher's steel. Set blades as close as possible, without the blades binding.

A pruning saw is ideal for cutting small branches, but it is hard work using one on live wood much more than 10 cm thick (for which either a bowsaw or chainsaw is more appropriate). The most effective design is slightly curved and cuts on the pull stroke. Pruning saws have specially designed teeth for cutting live wood, so a carpenter's saw is not a good substitute. Because of their shape pruning saws can only be hand sharpened, but with normal home use they will stay sharp for many years, especially if they are cleaned and oiled regularly.

Right: Sharp good-quality secateurs (for stems up to 15 mm in diameter) and a pair of strong protective gardening gloves are essential for pruning.

LIGHT-PRUNING GROUP

Plants in this group normally grow well and flower well with a minimum of intervention, but sometimes age or adverse circumstances can cause poor growth or dieback. With some of these species nothing can be done other than to replace them, while others may be revived by a single drastic pruning.

Much will depend on the specific variety under cultivation and the climatic conditions relating to the region. If in any doubt, consult your local nursery.

Below: Camellias.

SINGLE STEM WITH LATERAL SHOOTS

These shrubs can go many years with just grooming (including deadheading), some thinning of weaker shoots, and trimming to maintain a good natural shape. For a denser growth, pinch out tips in summer. Watch shrubs with variegated foliage for reversion: remove green shoots at source (but not green young shoots on purple pittosporums). Photinias need frequent light trimming to stimulate coloured young growth. Remove stock shoots from grafted subjects.

Many shrubs that are gaunt and spindly due to age or unfavourable environment can be cut back hard (camellias even to ground level) and will then sprout vigorously with the help of improved growing conditions. This treatment is not suitable for magnolias, maples, or conifers other than yews. Do not cut acacia to leafless wood.

THIS GROUP INCLUDES:

Acacia, arbutus, aucuba, box, broadleaf, camellia, choisya, conifers, coprosma, corokia, daphne, euonymus (evergreen kinds), garrya, gaultheria, holly, lilac, lophomyrtus, magnolia, maple, photinia, pieris, pittosporum and privet.

SINGLE STEM WITH BRANCHES THAT DIVIDE AFTER FLOWERING

Groom and deadhead these shrubs after flowering, and make sprawling plants more compact by pruning their outer branches.

For members of the Proteaceae family, cut spent flowers just below the flowerhead, or include the stalk to make growth more compact. A few proteas have live buds on the bare wood, which allows them to be cut back hard if they become straggly. The buds are usually prominent structures that may spontaneously produce new shoots from the base of old stems. For example, of the species commonly grown, live buds occur on the bare wood of *Protea cynaroïde* (king protea) and *Protea grandiceps*, but are absent from *Protea nerifolia*.

Deadhead rhododendrons by snapping off the inflorescence just below the head, avoiding damage to the buds. Old plants often become straggly and can be cut back hard, even cutting into leafless wood. Dormant buds are hidden by the bark, so expect to trim off some stubs later. Shorten unproductive azalea stems or cut them to the ground.

In warm regions, if you have either callistemon or beaufortia always prune to a whorl of branches, never to leafless wood. Untidy plants will benefit from thinning.

MULTIPLE STEMS

Fatsia, leucothoë, mahonias, nandinas and pseudopanax all have a tendency eventually to become leggy. Shoots may be cut back to the ground to stimulate new growth.

Below: Rhododendrons.

REGULAR DETAILED PRUNING

In all except cooler regions where frost determines plant survival, in most cases prune as soon as blooms fade (including plants that give several flushes, such as fuchsias and catmint).

Likewise, in the spring prune all berried shrubs and, if the climate permits growing on, half-hardy species such as hibiscus and lantana. Roses (see pp. 86-91) should be given a light pruning in late autumn before the ravages of frost and wind, then a heavier pruning in spring. South African ericas – mainly suited to milder regions, where they flower for most of the year – should be pruned or picked regularly (cut stems above a strong whorl of branches).

FLOWERING ON CURRENT SEASON'S GROWTH

Because they need to grow new wood before flowering, these shrubs seldom bloom until mid-summer. If left unpruned, they become leggy or crowded and prone to disease.

Prune deciduous varieties while dormant, but leave evergreens and half-hardy species until the spring. Very vigorous varieties may be cut down almost to ground level, leaving only two or three buds at the base of each stem – but for less vigorous species, or if a larger shrub is preferred, leave more length and in future seasons stub (cut back) shoots to two or three buds from this framework. After the first year, thin shoots out each season and stub back only the strongest.

Some shrubs do better if allowed to develop permanent leaders, which are only lightly tipped each year and whose side branches are stubbed back. Thin leaders out annually, replacing some with new shoots. Shrubs in this group include:

Below: Pruning a buddleia.

ABUTILON

Train permanent leaders, or for a smaller bush stub to a framework in spring.

BUDDLEIA (NOT *ALTERNIFOLIA* OR *GLOBOSA*)

Stub to the base or a framework in spring.

CARYOPTERIS

Stub to the base in spring.

CEANOTHUS

Cut deciduous varieties to within 8 cm of old wood in spring, but stub evergreens to leaders.

CERATOSTIGMA

Stub old or damaged shoots to the base in spring.

ESCALLONIA

Trim lightly to encourage flowering. After flowering has finished, remove flowered growth. Established escallonia hedges benefit from hard pruning.

FUCHSIA

Hardy fuchsias and, in mild areas, hybrids grown outdoors can be stubbed to the base either in late autumn or in spring. Remove all dead or diseased wood in the spring.

HIBISCUS (HARDY AND TROPICAL)

Stub back laterals to within 8 cm of old wood in spring. Long shoots may be shortened immediately after flowering.

LANTANA

If plants are grown on, prune main shoots back to 10 cm in early spring.

LAVENDULA (LAVENDER)

Remove dead flower stems and trim lavender lightly in late summer. Straggly plants can be cut back hard in spring to promote bushy growth.

Below: Pruning lavender.

LIPPIA (LEMON VERBENA)

If the plant is damaged by frost, new growth will usually appear from base. Stub to a framework about 30 cm above the ground in spring.

HYDRANGEA

Remove dead heads after flowering or in spring. Stub back shoots that are two to three years old, either to the ground or to create a framework.

Below: Hydrangea.

POTENTILLA

Keep bushy and vigorous by ground-level removal of weak or old stems.

BELOPERONE (SHRIMP PLANT – TROPICAL)

Reduce the main stems by half in early spring to maintain the shape.

SPARTIUM (SPANISH BROOM)

Remove dead flowerheads to prevent seeding. A light trim in autumn encourages flowering.

SPIRAEA X BUMALDA, SPIRAEA JAPONICA

Stub to within 8-10 cm of base in spring.

TAMARIX PENTANDRA

During the winter remove half to two thirds of the previous season's growth.

Roses belong in this group. Though commonly restricted by being grafted, they are true thickets, so stems regularly die but are replaced. For information on pruning roses see pp. 86-91.

FLOWERING ON PREVIOUS SEASON'S GROWTH

These shrubs mostly have a thicket habit, with stems flowering on the tip initially and thereafter on side shoots. After a first flowering cut stems back to a low, strong side shoot. For a year or two cut back to shoots that are low on stems which have flowered, but remove some old stems to encourage new growth from the base. Shrubs in this group include:

BUDDLEIA ALTERNIFOLIA, BUDDLEIA GLOBOSA

Prune to within 5-10cm of old wood.

DEUTZIA (TALL KINDS)

Remove old stems in late summer.

HYPERICUM

Prune to within a few centimetres of the base in spring every few years.

KERRIA

Cut to strong new growth after flowering.

PHILADELPHUS

Thin out old wood after flowering – but retain new growth, which will flower the following year.

RIBES SANGUINEUM (FLOWERING CURRANT)

Reduce stems by one-third in autumn.

SPIRAEA ARGUTA, WEIGELA

Weigela (all species) and *Spiraea arguta* need to be thinned occasionally. Remove one or two of the old stems after flowering, cutting them back to the base.

Below: Buddleia.

On non-thicket types prune away flower-heads and any weak or worn-out growth. Shrubs in this category include:

CYTISUS (BROOM)

Reduce by up to two-thirds after flowering.

CISTUS

Thin out damaged stems only.

HEBE

If leggy, cut back hard in spring to encourage new shoots from the base.

TAMARIX TETRANDRA

After flowering remove half to two-thirds of the previous season's growth.

Some plants needing special treatment are:

BERBERIS

Prune deciduous varieties in early spring, and evergreen varieties after flowering.

HEATHS AND EUROPEAN HEATHERS

Shear heads immediately after flowering, remove most of the current season's growth.

HYDRANGEA MACROPHYLLA

Thin out stems that are two to three years old at ground level, to encourage new shoots in spring.

LUCULIA

Reduce to 8 cm as flowers fade.

FLOWERING ON SPURS

Shrubs included in this group are:

CHAENOMELES JAPONICA

Becomes an unmanageable tangle if left untrained. On new plants select several well-balanced leaders and remove surplus shoots. Trim side shoots to three or four buds to encourage spur formation. Once flowering is established, requires only light trimming, thinning and shaping.

FORSYTHIA

A thicket; the first-year shoots are vegetative only, producing flowering spurs in the second. Remove old or damaged wood after flowering; on laterals cut back to one or two buds from the old wood.

PRUNING FOR FOLIAGE

On some deciduous shrubs the vigorous young foliage is the most spectacular, especially on the smoke tree (*Cotinus coggygria*). Prune straggly growth, either shortening or removing it, in late winter.

EUONYMUS (SPINDLE TREE)

Shoots can be thinned or shortened in late winter.

PAULOWNIA TOMENTOSA (EMPRESS TREE)

Cut to soil level each spring if grown as an accent shrub or pot plant; it will then have outsize velvety leaves, but no flowers.

Evergreens improved by cutting back hard in spring include:

TEUCRIUM FRUTICANS (SHRUBBY GERMANDER) AND *SANTOLINA* (COTTON LAVENDER)

In spring remove frost damaged tips and shorten growth by half to limit spread.

THYME

Clip thymes and most other herbs (see pp. 136-41) several times a year, to promote healthy growth.

Left: Clipping thyme.

FRUIT TREES

PIP FRUITS

Pip-fruit trees are spur-bearers, pruned mainly in winter during frost-free weather.

APPLES AND PEARS

These trees do not fruit until sufficiently mature. Some take up to twenty years, but grafting on suitable stock reduces the time to about two to three years for apples, a little longer for pears. As young trees find it hard to grow and crop, limit production until they have developed a sturdy framework. Initially, some varieties will only crop every second year.

Below: Pruning an apple tree using long-handled secateurs.

You sometimes find very large trees on older properties, but nowadays trees for home gardens are mostly on dwarfing stock – the apple trees generally reaching about 2 metres and pears between 3 and 4 metres, though they can be kept smaller.

The trees are often sold as whips (single stems) that can be trained as single-stem trees or pruned to a vase shape with several leaders, whereas trees that are already branched are suitable only for multiple-stem growing. While apples can be grown either way, most amateurs find it easiest to manage pear trees with several leaders.

FRAMEWORK DEVELOPMENT

For a vase shape, the first pruning will depend on whether the tree is a whip or already branched.

1 In order to branch, whips must be decapitated at a suitable height and all the top buds left to grow. A year's growth will produce several branches, and three strong ones should be chosen. These should not make a narrow angle with the trunk, or they may split later.

2 Cut back hard. At the tip leave buds that face sideways rather than straight out or in. Remove all other shoots.

3 After one more year, select from four to six even-sized shoots well spaced around the tree and remove all other upright growth.

One leader or several are treated the same from now on. The aim is to develop a series of side branches (fruiting arms) at regular intervals, that will support fruiting wood. Where there is a single leader these limbs emerge all around the main trunk, but with multiple leaders inward-turning branches are removed, letting light and air into the centre.

TO DEVELOP SIDE SHOOTS

1 Decapitate stems just above the height where you want a branch. The top bud will become a new leader, and the second bud should be destroyed. The next bud or buds will grow out to form limbs, which may be thinned if too close.

2 Repeat this process annually until the tree has reached the required height.

3 Then cut back the leader to a weak side branch. If this weak shoot is not pruned, its

growth will be minimal and the height may be held for several years.

Strong shoots sometimes develop further down the stem, taking over as substitute leaders. These should always be cut away, leaving only the weak tip shoot.

The fruiting arms ought to be lightly pruned each winter. If they grow fairly flat, encourage this by cutting to an under-side bud – but in some apples and most pears they have a strong urge to turn up. This can be combated by tying down for a few months or by pruning as shown. When they reach the required spread, stop the growth at a weak side branch, as described for leaders.

Any wood that remains for more than one year on an apple or pear tree carries vegetative buds which have not grown out into branches and may be transformed into fruit buds. In the first year of their development they are simple, torpedo-shaped structures protruding from branches much more prominently than vegetative buds. Each is capable of giving rise to a cluster of blossoms and, ultimately, fruit.

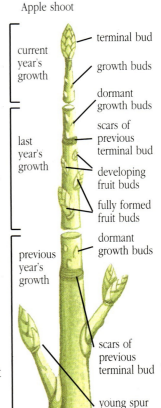

Apple shoot

current year's growth
- terminal bud
- growth buds
- dormant growth buds

last year's growth
- scars of previous terminal bud
- developing fruit buds
- fully formed fruit buds

previous year's growth
- dormant growth buds
- scars of previous terminal bud
- young spur

If the tip of the shoot has been cut, the bud nearest the cut end may also grow a new long shoot, but the majority of buds will develop into spurs. These are very compressed shoots that gradually evolve into branch structures, with each branch ending in one or two fruit buds. Spurs are usually very long-lived. Those that form on the main trunk when the tree is first planted may continue to survive after the tree has reached full maturity.

As spurs become increasingly branched, the quality of fruit they produce falls off due to competition between the buds. Every two or three years the majority of buds should be pruned away, leaving only two or three of the strongest. Spurs on the main trunk or major branches of older trees rarely produce good fruit, since they suffer from poor sap supply and lack of light, so should be removed completely.

It is possible to identify unthrifty spurs during the summer when the fruit is approaching maturity. Examine inner the parts of the tree, looking for bunches of fruit that are either smaller than normal or diseased or poorly coloured, then prune the unwanted spurs flush with the branch.

The main crop on mature trees is borne on twigs springing from fruiting arms. These should be allowed to grow uncut for two years and then be pruned back to where fruit buds have developed. If they are very long they should be shortened further, leaving only eight to ten buds. The end bud is likely to shoot during summer, and at the next pruning this shoot should be shortened to one or two buds. This procedure will need to be repeated again at subsequent prunings.

Below: Summer pruning of apples.

On less vigorous trees, leaving all the fruiting shoots may result in a crop of undersized fruit. If this happens, prune about one third of the shoots completely, leaving the remainder evenly spaced. Next summer check that enough wood has been removed.

After a few years some of the spurs may die, reducing the fruit crop. Cropping can often be improved by renewed pruning. At the base of each fruiting shoot are two or three tiny, dormant vegetative buds. If the rest of the shoot is removed, one or more of the buds will be stimulated to grow, so that new wood will be formed. During the next winter select the strongest new growth and remove the others.

A few apple trees (among them 'Rome Beauty' and 'Irish Peach') are tip bearers. Unpruned twigs develop fruit buds at the tips only, but if new laterals more than 10 cm long are cut back to about three buds, they will often be stimulated to develop fruit. Alternatively, strong laterals may be tied down so that their tips are lower than their bases, which will also stimulate extra fruit-bud formation.

Established dwarf apple trees usually need little pruning, but remove any twigs cluttering the inside of the tree, as well as damaged, downward-turning or crossing wood. The quality of the crop will indicate whether any further pruning is necessary. If the fruit is of a good quality, no more pruning is needed – whereas undersized fruit implies that there are too many buds. To reduce their number, thin the fruiting wood, remove ill-placed spurs and prune old many-branched spurs.

So-called dwarf pear trees (grafted onto quince stocks) are much more vigorous than dwarf apple trees. Although they are easier to manage than full-sized trees, they require similar pruning.

QUINCES

These are not as vigorous as apple or pear trees. They are best grown as vase shaped trees with many leaders and no fruiting arms. Fruit grows only on new wood at the tips of the shoots, so each year cut about a third of the shoots back hard to encourage new growth and leave the remainder uncut to produce the crop. This method prevents the tree from becoming too tall.

FLATTENING A LATERAL
BY PRUNING

A. (first pruning)

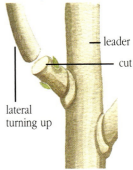

leader

cut

lateral
turning up

B. (second pruning)

strong,
upright growth
from
top bud

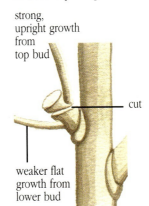

cut

weaker flat
growth from
lower bud

STONE FRUITS

There is no effective way of dwarfing this group – the few genetic dwarfs that exist produce inferior fruit.

Some stone-fruit trees tend to produce strong water shoots from lower branches. In normal circumstances these should be removed completely – but in decrepit peaches they may be grown into a new tree, cutting the rest away.

Carry out major pruning in summer straight after fruiting, to minimise the risk of deadly silverleaf disease.

Below: 'Grove's Late Victoria' plum in fruit.

PEACHES AND NECTARINES

Trees in warm regions need little pruning beyond the removal of any strong growth near the top; but in cold climates a lot of extra buds grow, necessitating thinning. Train on a single stem, and each year remove strong early-season growth, leaving the later-formed weaker wood, which fruits better.

Fruit only develops on pale reddish-brown growth of the current year. Heavy bearers should be winter-pruned as well, thinning out up to half the fruiting twigs and shortening the remainder.

PLUMS

Plums normally grow best pruned in a vase shape.

European plums: Select leaders, cut out excess shoots, and leave unpruned for a year or two until established. Fruit is borne on long-lived spurs. Each summer shorten strong young shoots as necessary to control height, and remove any dead, overcrowded or crossed laterals.

CHERRIES

Prune minimally once a framework is established. Some trees may need annual work to control size.

APRICOTS

Plump fruiting spurs form on one-year-old wood and last three or four years. Remove unfruitful wood annually. Pruning laterals in the summer will encourage spur formation.

CITRUS FRUITS

In warm regions these grow naturally into well-shaped trees, although some produce unwanted water shoots on the stem, close to the main branches.

Pruning can be done at any time except when frost is expected. After harvesting is the most convenient time to prune.

ORANGE AND GRAPEFRUITS

In warm regions established orange and grapefruit trees need little pruning beyond removal of water shoots and dead or diseased wood. 'Wheeny' grapefruit trees may benefit from being topped if they show a tendency to biennial bearing.

LEMONS AND MANDARINS

In warm regions 'Eureka' lemons sometimes have spindly, naked branches, which should be shortened. Other dense bushy types, like 'Meyer', and mandarins such as 'Clementine' or 'Thorny' benefit from a moderate thinning of fruit-bearing wood.

To revive aging citrus trees, remove older wood. Since fruiting laterals are slow to develop from cut ends, either thin out the laterals along a branch or shorten it to a lateral rather than a dormant bud.

Below: Orange trees are best pruned when there is no chance of frost and preferably after harvest.

HEDGEROW FRUITS

BLACKCURRANTS

Cut out wood that has fruited. Retain new, smooth, whitish shoots, especially coming from the base.

REDCURRANTS

Grow redcurrants on a single main stem with eight to twelve leaders. Stub back all laterals in winter to induce spur formation.

GOOSEBERRIES

Train as an open bush, removing crossing shoots and pruning out older wood each winter, when leaders should be cut back by half. In mid-summer prune all new laterals to five leaves, then shorten in winter to two buds.

RASPBERRIES

Either bunch and tie canes or grow them between wires or strings. After mid-summer cut all canes that have fruited to the ground and tie new growth. Thin new canes in winter and tip lightly.

BLACKBERRIES

These are usually grown on two or more parallel wires held by stout posts.

Remove canes that have fruited immediately after fruiting. Bunch and tie new summer growth.

GRAPEVINES

Avoid spring pruning, since it will cause copious bleeding.

Grapevines should be trained on two horizontal wires, about 60 cm apart. Tie the young vine to a stake. Decapitate it in winter just above the lower wire. The top bud will grow into a new leader, and the next two shoots that develop should be trained along the wire in opposite directions to form two fruiting rods. When the new leader reaches the second wire, it should be decapitated in turn and the two topmost shoots that develop trained as a second pair of rods.

Side shoots eventually bear fruit. During summer pinch fruiting shoots to two leaves beyond the bunch and shorten all non-fruiting wood to 50 cm, repeating as necessary. In winter stub back all laterals to two buds.

If a rod becomes unfruitful with age, choose a lateral as close to the main stem as possible and let this shoot grow unpruned all summer, tying it loosely to the old rod. During the winter prune away the old growth and tie the replacement rod to the wires.

MISCELLANEOUS

WISTARIA

Either grow wistaria freely over an old tree or train the rods on a wall. Cut side shoots to about 20 cm long in summer; then shorten in winter to four or five buds, to form spurs. Cut off surplus basal shoots during summer.

ESPALIERS

These are time-consuming and require patience. Espaliers are bushes or trees trained in two dimensions. They can be used ornamentally, or to save space or give wall protection to tender shrubs.

If your regional climate is too hot and dry for training against a brick or stone wall, fruit trees (both pip and stone fruits) can be trained against a wooden fence or on free-standing wires.

Use up to five horizontal wires training either parallel side shoots like a grapevine (pip fruits only) or upright shoots in a fan or gridiron configuration. Retain only shoots parallel with the wall.

On pip fruits only young growth is supple enough to train, so tie in the shoots loosely as they grow. During summer cut out any unwanted strong shoots and shorten the rest to 12 cm, cutting back to three buds in winter. Next season these should

form fruit buds. On older trees, renew unfruitful laterals by cutting back to basal buds.

Pyracanthas can be espaliered without supports, simply by pinching all forward-pointing shoots.

BOUGAINVILLEA

Bougainvilleas enjoy a hot wall. Train a permanent framework by pinching out unwanted shoots in summer and cutting back side shoots to two buds in the spring.

TREES

Remove any stray shoots with secateurs or shear lightly. Many conifers look more attractive if the bottom branches are retained. Shorten vertical growth by removing tiers of branches.

OTHERS

If trees have to be tailored to fit a restricted area, curtail growth early enough to avoid major surgery.

To form a standard, remove bottom branches progressively, so as not to deprive the young tree of too much nourishment. Some trees are sold as standards that are already prepared.

If the trees in your garden are casting excessive shade, let more light in by thinning rather than by mutilating them with decapitation.

INDEX